D1569924

# THE
# INDUSTRIAL
# REVOLUTION

## STEAM AND STEEL

EDITED BY
## JAMES WOLFE

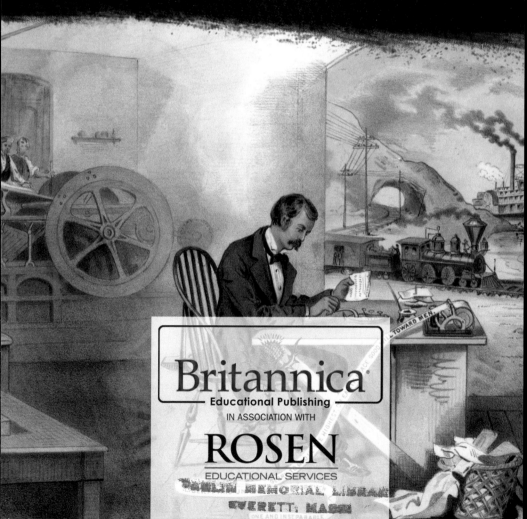

**Britannica**
Educational Publishing
IN ASSOCIATION WITH

## ROSEN
EDUCATIONAL SERVICES

YA

Published in 2016 by Britannica Educational Publishing (a trademark of Encyclopædia Britannica, Inc.) in association with The Rosen Publishing Group, Inc.
29 East 21st Street, New York, NY 10010

First Edition

*330.94*
*W85531*

**Britannica Educational Publishing**
J. E. Luebering: Director, Core Reference Group
Anthony L. Green: Editor, Compton's by Britannica

**Rosen Publishing**
Hope Lourie Killcoyne: Executive Editor
Christine Poolos: Editor
Nelson Sá: Art Director
Brian Garvey: Designer
Cindy Reiman: Photography Manager

**Library of Congress Cataloging-in-Publication Data**

The Industrial Revolution : steam and steel/edited by James Wolfe.—First edition.
    pages cm.—(The age of revolution)
Includes bibliographical references and index.
ISBN 978-1-68048-026-9 (library bound)
1. Industrial revolution—Europe—Juvenile literature. 2. Industrial revolution—United States—Juvenile literature. 3. Industrialization—Europe—History—Juvenile literature. 4. Industrialization—United States—History—Juvenile literature. 5. Technological innovations—Social aspects—Europe—History—Juvenile literature. 6. Technological innovations—Social aspects—United States—History—Juvenile literature. 7. Europe—Economic conditions—Juvenile literature. 8. United States—Economic conditions—Juvenile literature. I. Wolfe, James, 1960–
HC240.I5334 2016
330.94'028—dc23

                                                                    2014040493

*Manufactured in the United States of America*

**Photo credits:** Cover, p. 1 Everett Historical/Shutterstock.com; pp. viii–ix Library of Congress, Washington, D.C. (digital no. 3b11564); p. 3 DeAgostini/SuperStock; p. 7 The Granger Collection, New York; p. 11 Heritage Images/Hulton Fine Art Collection/Getty Images; p. 22 Universal History Archive/UIG/Bridgeman Images; p. 27 Courtesy of the Bibliothèque de l'Institut de France, Paris; photograph, The Science Museum, London; pp. 30, 54 © Photos.com/Jupiterimages; p. 33 De Agostini Picture Library/Getty Images; p. 38 BBC Hulton Picture Library; p. 41 © Comstock Images/Jupiterimages; pp. 48–49 DEA/S. Vannini/De Agostini/Getty Images; p. 52 © Photos.com/Thinkstock pp. 59, 67, 148 Library of Congress, Washington, D.C.; pp. 62–63 Neue Nationalgalerie, Berlin, Germany/Bridgeman Images; p. 82 DEA/G. Dagli Orti/De Agostini/Getty Images; pp. 84–85 Private Collection/© Look and Learn/Bridgeman Images; pp. 88–89 Science & Society Picture Library/Getty Images; p. 92 Keystone-France/Gamma-Keystone/Getty Images; pp. 101, 136 Encyclopædia Britannica, Inc.; p. 108 FPG/Archive Photos/Getty Images; p. 110 Popperfoto/Getty Images; p. 119 British Crown copyright, Science Museum, London; pp. 127, 134 Print Collector/Hulton Archive/Getty Images; p. 143 Danita Delimont/Gallo Images/Getty Images; p. 147 Prints and Photographs Division/Library of Congress, Washington, D.C. (LC-USZ62-1342).

# CONTENTS

# CONTENTS

## CHAPTER 3

## THE INDUSTRIAL REVOLUTION
## BEGINS IN ENGLAND

# CONTENTS

## CHAPTER 4

# THE SECOND INDUSTRIAL REVOLUTION AND A CHANGING SOCIETY . . . . . . . . . . . . . . . 86

# CONTENTS

In modern history, the Industrial Revolution refers to the process of change from an agrarian, handicraft economy to one dominated by industry and machine manufacture. This process began in England in the 18th century and from there spread to other parts of the world. Although used earlier by French writers, the term "Industrial Revolution" was first popularized by the English economic historian Arnold Toynbee (1852–83) to describe England's economic development from 1760 to 1840. Since Toynbee's time the term has been more broadly applied.

It is almost impossible to imagine what the world would be like if the effects of the Industrial Revolution were swept away. Electric lights would go out. Automobiles and airplanes would vanish. Telephones, radios, and television would disappear. Most of the abundant stocks on the shelves of department stores would be gone. The children of the poor would have little or no schooling and would work from dawn to dark on the farm or in the home. Before machines were invented, work by children as well as by adults was needed in order to provide enough food, clothing, and shelter for all.

The main features involved in the Industrial Revolution were technological, socioeconomic, and cultural changes. The technological changes included the following: (1) the use of new basic materials, chiefly iron and steel, (2) the use of new energy sources, including both fuels and motive power, such as coal,

*Completed Ford Model Ts come off the Ford Motor Company assembly line in Detroit, Michigan, in about 1917.*

the steam engine, electricity, petroleum, and the internal-combustion engine, (3) the invention of new machines, such as the spinning jenny and the power loom, which permitted increased production with a smaller expenditure of human energy, (4) a new organization of work known as the factory system, which entailed increased division of labour and specialization of function, (5) important developments in transportation and communication, including the steam locomotive, steamship, automobile, airplane, telegraph, and radio, and (6) the increasing application of science to industry. These technological changes made possible a tremendously increased use of natural resources and the mass production of manufactured goods.

There were also many new developments in nonindustrial spheres, including the following: (1) agricultural improvements that made possible the provision of food for a larger nonagricultural population, (2) economic changes that resulted in a wider distribution of wealth, the decline of land as a source of wealth in the face of rising industrial production, and increased international trade, (3) political changes reflecting the shift in economic power, as well as new state policies corresponding to the needs of an industrialized society, (4) sweeping social changes, including the growth of cities, the development of working-class movements, and the emergence of new patterns of authority, and (5) cultural transformations of a broad order. The worker acquired new and distinctive skills, and his relation to his task shifted; instead of being a craftsman working with hand tools, he became a machine operator, subject to factory discipline.

Finally, there was a psychological change: man's confidence in his ability to use resources and to master nature was heightened.

# THE FIRST INDUSTRIAL REVOLUTION

In the period 1760 to 1830 the Industrial Revolution was largely confined to Britain. Aware of their head start, the British forbade the export of machinery, skilled workers, and manufacturing techniques. The British monopoly could not last forever, especially since some Britons saw profitable industrial opportunities abroad, while continental European businessmen sought to lure British know-how to their countries. Two Englishmen, William and John Cockerill, brought the Industrial Revolution to Belgium by developing machine shops at Liège (c. 1807), and Belgium became the first country in continental Europe to be transformed economically. Like its English progenitor, the Belgian Industrial Revolution centred in iron, coal, and textiles.

France was more slowly and less thoroughly industrialized than either Britain or Belgium. While Britain was establishing its industrial leadership, France was immersed in its Revolution, and the uncertain political situation discouraged large investments in industrial innovations. By 1848 France had become an industrial power, but, despite great growth under the Second Empire, it remained behind England.

Other European countries lagged far behind. Their bourgeoisie lacked the wealth, power, and opportunities of their British, French, and Belgian counterparts. Political conditions in the other nations also hindered industrial expansion. Germany, for example, despite vast resources of coal and iron, did not begin its industrial expansion until after national unity was achieved in 1870. Once begun, Germany's industrial production grew so rapidly that by the turn of the century that nation was outproducing Britain in steel and had become the world leader in the chemical industries. The rise of U.S. industrial power in the 19th and 20th centuries also far outstripped European efforts. And Japan too joined the Industrial Revolution with striking success.

The eastern European countries were behind early in the 20th century. It was not until the five-year plans that the Soviet Union became a major industrial power, telescoping into a few decades the industrialization that had taken a century and a half in Britain. The mid-20th century witnessed the spread of the Industrial Revolution into hitherto nonindustrialized areas such as China and India.

# THE SECOND INDUSTRIAL REVOLUTION

Despite considerable overlapping with the "old," there is mounting evidence for a "new" Industrial Revolution in the late 19th and 20th centuries. In terms of basic materials, modern industry has begun to exploit many natural and synthetic resources not hitherto utilized: lighter metals, new alloys, and synthetic products such as plastics, as well as new energy sources. Combined with these are developments in machines, tools, and computers that have given rise to the automatic factory. Although some segments of industry were almost completely mechanized in the early to mid-19th century, automatic operation, as distinct from the assembly line, first achieved major significance in the second half of the 20th century.

Ownership of the means of production also underwent changes. The oligarchical ownership of the means of production that characterized the Industrial Revolution in the early to mid-19th century gave way to a wider distribution of ownership through purchase of common stocks by individuals and by institutions such as insurance companies. In the 20th century, many countries of Europe socialized basic sectors of their economies. There was also a change in political theories: instead of the laissez-faire ideas that dominated the economic and social thought of the classical Industrial Revolution, governments generally moved into the social and economic realm to meet the needs of their more complex industrial societies.

## A MODERN SOCIETY

The Industrial Revolution in Great Britain laid down the economic pattern of the modern world. It also brought revolutionary changes to society. The share of men employed in agriculture fell from 60 percent to about 25 percent, while the share of those employed in industry rose from less than 20 percent to nearly 50 percent. Between 1700 and 1850, England's population surged from between 6 and 7 million to nearly 21 million. Industrial output, which had increased by less than 1 percent per year in the first half of the 18th century, was rising by nearly 3 percent per year by the early part of the 19th century. The changes that took place in Britain during the 19th century served as an effective prototype of industrialization. To choose to industrialize—and not to choose meant risking backwardness and dependence—was to imitate consciously the British Industrial Revolution. Great Britain was the pioneer industrial nation of the world;

there simply was no other model to fix on. Even later, when it was clear that the British method of industrialization might not be exclusively valid or universally applicable, the general form of society that emerged in the course of the Industrial Revolution was widely regarded as typical.

Certain episodes and tendencies in the British case were pointed to as characterizing industrial development as such. These included the movement from the land to the cities, the massing of workers in the new industrial towns and factories, and the rise of new distinctions between family life and work life, and between work and leisure as notions meaningful to large classes of persons. Such features, with various others, were compounded into a powerful image of industrialism as a whole and wholly new social system and way of life.

Although the progress brought about by the Industrial Revolution is generally considered to be positive, the movement is responsible for introducing several negative consequences to the health of the population and the planet. Rapid technological progress and industrial growth had led to crowded, unsanitary working and living conditions, with a corresponding rise in the number of accidents and deaths caused by the new machinery and exposure to toxic materials. In 1775 Percivall Pott, a London surgeon, linked the frequent occurrence of scrotal cancer among chimney sweeps to the soot ingrained into their skin by prolonged exposure to flue dusts. Charles Turner Thackrah, a Leeds physician, further advanced the study of occupational medicine in Britain with his *The Effects of the Principal Arts, Trades and Professions . . . on Health and Longevity . . .* (1831), which described lung diseases caused by dust that commonly afflicted miners and metal grinders. In 1895 Britain introduced a statutory notification system that required medical personnel to report all occurrences of certain diseases to the chief inspector of factories. Other industrial nations followed Britain's lead, and legal provisions for the health of the worker continued to be instituted throughout the 19th and 20th centuries. In addition, industrialization has been linked to steady increases in greenhouse gases responsible for severe climate change. Countries in North America and Europe that were the first to undergo the process of industrialization have been responsible for releasing the most greenhouse gases in absolute cumulative terms since the beginning of the Industrial Revolution.

In today's Information Age, a preindustrial world can seem like life on another planet. Before computers, before assembly lines, before globalization, lived a mostly uneducated society that had no knowledge of goings-on in the rest of the world. This volume examines the Industrial Revolution and its far-reaching effects on society. The first two chapters attempt to describe that world, approaching preindustrial Europe from historical, sociological, economic, and technological points of view. The next two chapters describe the first and second Industrial Revolutions in compelling detail. The final chapter delves into the many inventions and developments of this period, putting into context their contributions to the advancement of technology.

## CHAPTER 1

# SOCIETY BEFORE THE INDUSTRIAL REVOLUTION

To fully grasp the impact of the Industrial Revolution, it is important to understand what life was like before it occurred. Seventeenth-century Europe was entirely different from what we know today. For most inhabitants, the highest aim was to survive in a hazardous world. They were contained in an inelastic frame by their inability to produce more than a certain amount of food or to make goods except by hand or using relatively simple tools and machines.

## THE HUMAN CONDITION

In this natural, or preindustrial, economy, the human population played the main part in determining production and demand through the amount of labour available for field, mill, and workshop and through the number of consumers. Quality of life was determined in great part by the most basic needs.

## HEALTH AND SICKNESS

Disease was ever present, ready to take advantage of feeble defense systems operating without the benefit of science. The 20th-century French historian Robert Mandrou wrote of "the chronic morbidity" of the entire population.

Vaccination was not much used until the beginning of the 19th century. As in other scientific fields, there was a long pause between pioneering research and regular practice. Trained by book, taking no account of organic life, envisaging illness as a foreign element lodged in the sick person's body, even tending to identify disease with sin, doctors prescribed, dosed, and bled, leaning on pedantic scholarship blended with primitive psychology. Therapy was concerned mainly with moderating symptoms.

To peer in imagination into the hovels of the poor or to walk down streets with open drains between houses decayed into crowded tenements, is to understand why mortality rates among the poor were so high. In town and country they lived in one or two rooms, often under the same roof as their animals, sleeping on straw, eating with their fingers or with a knife and spoon, washing infrequently, and tolerating lice and fleas. Outside, dung and refuse attracted flies and rodents. Luckier people, particularly in the north, might have had glass in their windows, but light was less important than warmth. In airless rooms, thick with the odours of dampness,

*THIS ARTWORK DEPICTS PEOPLE LINING UP TO RECEIVE SMALLPOX VACCINATIONS IN FRANCE. SMALLPOX WAS ONE OF THE FIRST DISEASES TO BE CONTROLLED BY VACCINE.*

defecation, smoke, and unwashed bodies, rheumatic or bronchial ailments might be the least of troubles. Deficient diet in childhood could mean rickety legs. Crude methods of delivery might cause permanent damage to both mothers and children who survived the attentions of the local midwife. The baby who survived (one in four died in the first year of life) was launched on a hazardous journey.

Some diseases, such as measles, seem to have been more virulent then than now. Typhus, spread by lice and fleas, and typhoid, which was waterborne, killed many. Syphilis had been a growing menace since its introduction in the 16th century, and it was rife among prostitutes and their patrons: it was a common cause of blindness in children. Women, hapless victims of male-dominated morality, were frequently denied the chance of early mercury treatment because of the stigma attached to the disease. Scrofula, a gangrenous tubercular condition of the lymph glands, was known as "the king's evil" because it was thought to be curable by the king's touch: Louis XIV practiced the ceremony conscientiously. Malaria was endemic in some swampy areas. Though drainage schemes were taken up by enlightened sovereigns, prevention awaited inexpensive quinine. Nor could doctors do more than let smallpox take its course before the general introduction of vaccines. The plague, chiefly an urban disease that was deadliest in summer and dreaded as a sentence of death, could be combated only by measures of quarantine.

## POVERTY

Poverty was a constant state. If those with sufficient land or a wage large enough to allow for the replacement of tools and stock are held to be above the poverty line, then at least a quarter of Europe's inhabitants were below it. The philosopher the Marquis de Condorcet described those who "possess neither goods nor chattels [and are] destined to fall into misery at the least accident." That could be illness or injury to a breadwinner, the failure of a crop or death of a cow, fire or flood, or the death or bankruptcy of an employer. Taxes, on top of rents and dues, might be the decisive factor in the slide from sufficiency to destitution.

Urban poverty posed the biggest threat to governments. The situation became alarming after 1750 because the rise in population forced food prices up, while the employers' advantage in the labour market depressed wages. The typical relationship of mutual support was between poor hill country and large town. Younger sons from the European fringes went for bread to the big armies. Women were usually left behind with the old men and children to look after the harvest in areas of seasonal migration. Domestic service drew many girls to towns with a large bourgeois population. Certain other occupations, notably lacemaking, were traditionally reserved for women. Miserably paid, young Frenchwomen risked their eyesight in fine work to earn enough for dowry and marriage. In a society where contraception was little known, except through abstinence, and irregular liaisons were frowned upon, the tendency to marry late was an indication of poverty. Almost half the women of western Europe married after 25; between 10 and 15 percent did not marry at all. The prevalence of abortion and infanticide is painfully significant: it was clearly not confined to unmarried couples. In 18th-century Brussels, more than 2,000 babies were abandoned annually to be looked after by charitable institutions. Every major city had large numbers of prostitutes. Victims and outcasts, with the beggars and derelicts of crowded tenements, they helped create the amoral ambience in which criminals could expect tolerance and shelter.

Barred by magistrates from the towns, gangs of beggars terrorized country districts. Children, pursuing victims with sorry tales, were keen trainees in the school of crime, picking pockets, cutting horsetails, soliciting for "sisters," and abetting smuggling. The enlargement of the role of the state, with tariffs as the main weapon in protectionist strategies, encouraged evasion and smuggling.

# THE ORGANIZATION OF SOCIETY

European society was rigid, with few rights for most and little opportunity to advance from the place into which citizens were born.

## CORPORATE SOCIETY

Feudalism, as a set of political arrangements, was dead by 1600. But aspects of feudal society survived, notably in the countryside. Various forms of personal service were owed by peasants to landowners and, in armies and courts, assumption of office and terms of service reflected the dealings of earlier times when power lay in the ownership of land. Envisaging such a society, the reader must dismiss the idea of natural rights, which was not current until the last decades of the 18th century. Rights accrued by virtue of belonging, in two ways: first, as the subject of a prince or equivalent authority—for example, magistrates of a free town or the bishop of an ecclesiastical principality; second, as the member of a community or corporation, in which one had rights depending on the rank into which one was born or on one's craft or profession.

The family was the lifeblood of all associations, giving purpose and identity to people who were rarely in crowds and knew nothing like the large, impersonal organization of modern times. The intimacies of domestic life could not anesthetize against pain and hunger: life was not softened and death was a familiar visitor. Children were

*A PAINTING SHOWS SERFS GIVING ANIMALS TO THEIR LORD.*

especially vulnerable but enjoyed no special status. Valued as an extra pair of hands or deplored as an extra mouth to feed, the child belonged to no privileged realm of play and protection from life's responsibilities. The family might be extended by numerous relations living nearby. Especially in more isolated communities, inbreeding added genetic hazards to the struggle for life.

Everywhere the hold of the family, and of the father over the family, strengthened by laws of property and inheritance, curtained life's narrow windows from glimpses of a freer world. It affected marriage, since land, business, and dowry were customarily of more weight than the feelings of

## FEUDALISM

Before the rise of national states in western Europe, the people lived under a system called feudalism. This was a social system of rights and obligations based on land ownership patterns.

Each small district was ruled by a duke, count, or other noble. The noble's power was based on the land he held in feud. This peculiar system of landholding determined the pattern of government. It also gave rise to fortified castles, knights in armor, and chivalry. The term "feudalism" therefore describes an entire way of life.

The system of feudalism was established gradually, between the 8th and 11th centuries. France was the land of its earliest and most complete development, but in some form or other it was found in all the countries of western Europe. It flourished especially from the 11th to the end of the 13th century. There are survivals of feudalism in the laws and social usages of modern European countries.

the bride and groom. But into dowries and ceremonies long saved for would go the display required to sustain the family name.

## NOBLES AND GENTLEMEN

Between persistent poverty and the prevailing aristocratic spirit several connections can be made. The strong appeal of noble status and values was a force working generally against the pursuit of wealth and the investment that was to lead, precociously and exceptionally in Britain, to the Industrial Revolution. The typical relationship between landed gentleman and peasant producer was still feudal; whether represented by a range of rights and dues or by the more rigorous form of serfdom, it encouraged acceptance of the status quo in agriculture. Possession of land was a characteristic mark and aspiration of the elites.

Landowners enjoyed rights over peasants, not least as judge in their own court. In France, parts of Germany, Italy, and Spain, even if one did not own the land, he could as lord still benefit from feudal dues. He could hope for special favours from his sovereign or other patron in the form of a pension or office. There were vital exemptions, as from billeting soldiers and— most valuable—from taxation. Generally they could expect favourable treatment: special schools, privileges at university, preferment in the church, commissions in the army. They could assume that a sovereign, while encroaching on their rights, would yet share their values. The decline of Continental estates and diets, with the growth of bureaucracies, largely recruited from commoners, did not mean, however, even in the west, that nobility was in retreat before the rise of the bourgeoisie. Through social preeminence, nobles maintained—and in the 18th century even tightened—their hold on the commanding heights in church and state. Status increasingly signified economic circumstances.

Nobility also had a civilizing role. Europe would be immeasurably poorer without the music, literature, and architecture of the age of aristocracy. The virtues of classical taste were to some extent those of aristocracy: splendour restrained by formal rules and love of beauty uninhibited by utilitarian considerations.

## THE BOURGEOISIE

The European bourgeoisie presents faces so different that common traits can be discerned only at the simplest level: the possession of property with the desire and means to increase it, emancipation from past precepts about investment, a readiness to work for a living, and a sense of being superior to town workers or peasants. With their social values—sobriety, discretion, and economy—went a tendency to imitate the style of their social superiors.

A universal phenomenon was the growth of capital cities, which benefited from the expansion of government, particularly if, as was usual, the court was within the city. Growth could acquire its own momentum, irrespective of the condition of the country: besides clients and servants of all kinds, artisans, shopkeepers, and other providers of services swelled the ranks.

Other cities grew around specialized industries or from opportunities for a wider trade than was possible where markets were limited by the range of horse and mule. Enterprise brought remarkable growth in Britain, where Manchester and Birmingham both moved up from modest beginnings to the 100,000-population mark during the 18th century. Atlantic ports thrived during the same period with the increase in colonial trade.

A typical urban experience, where there was no special factor at work, was therefore one of stability. The burgher of 1600 would have felt at home in the town of his descendant five generations later. There was a special kind of deadness about towns that had no other raison d'être than to be host to

**10**

BEER STREET.

WITH AN INCREASE IN TRADE, MANY EUROPEAN TOWNS EXPANDED AND A MIDDLE CLASS EMERGED, WILLING TO SPEND WAGES ON FOOD, DRINK, AND GOODS.

numerous clergy. Most numerous were the quiet places that had never grown from their basic function of providing a market.

Between these extremes lay the mass of towns of middling size, each supervised by a mayor and corporation, dignified by one large church and probably several others serving ward or parish, and including a law court, guildhall, school, and, of course, market. With its bourgeois crust of clerics, lawyers, officials, merchants, and shopkeepers and master craftsmen catering for special needs—fine fabrics, clothing, hats, wigs, gloves, eyeglasses, engravings if not paintings, china, silver, glassware, locks, and clocks—the city was a world apart from the peasant. The contrast was emphasized by the walls, the gates that closed at night, the cobbles or setts of the roads, the different speech and intonation, the well-fed look of some citizens, and above all the fine houses, suggesting as much an ordered way of life as the wealth that supported it.

Within towns, popular forms of government were abandoned as power was monopolized by groups of wealthy men. Everywhere elites were composed of those who had no business role. A more serious threat to the old urban regime lay in another area where discontents bred radicalism: the guilds. They became more restrictive in the face of competition and growing numbers of would-be members and so drove industries, particularly those suited to dispersed production, back to the countryside. To compensate for falling production, masters tended to put pressure on the relatively unskilled level, where there were always more workers than work. Journeymen's associations sought to improve their situation, sometimes through strikes. The building trade was notorious for its secret societies. The decline of the guilds was only one symptom of the rise in population. Another was the rise in urban poverty, as pressure on resources led to price increases that outstripped wages. The plight of the poor was emphasized by the affluence of increasing numbers of fellow citizens. However class conflict is interpreted, it is clear that its basic elements were by that time present and active.

## THE PEASANTRY

The peasant's life was conditioned by mundane factors: soil, water supplies, communications, and above all the site itself in relation to river, sea, frontier, or strategic route. The community could be virtually self-sufficient. Its environment was formed by what could be bred, fed, sown, gathered, and worked within the bounds of the parish. Fields and beasts provided food and clothing; wood came from the fringe of wasteland. Except in districts where stone was available and easy to work, houses were usually made of wood or a cob of clay and straw. Intended to provide shelter from the elements, they can be envisaged as a refinement of the barn, with certain amenities for their human occupants: hearth, table, and benches with mats and rushes strewn on a floor of beaten earth or rough stone. Generally there would be a single story, with a raised space for beds and an attic for grain. For his own warmth and their security the peasant slept close to his animals, under the same roof. Cooking required an iron pot, sometimes the only utensil named in peasant inventories. Meals were eaten off wood or earthenware. Fuel was normally wood, which was becoming scarce in some intensively cultivated parts of northern Europe, particularly Holland, where much of the land was reclaimed from sea or marsh. Peat and dried dung also were used, but rarely coal.

Corn was ground at the village mill, a place of potential conflict: only one man had the necessary expertise, and his clients were poorly placed to bargain. Women and girls spun and wove for the itinerant merchants who supplied the wool or simply for the household, for breeches, shirts, tunics, smocks, and gowns. Clothes served elemental needs: they were usually thick for protection against damp and cold and loose-fitting for ease of movement. Shoes were likely to be wooden clogs, as leather was needed for harnesses. Farm implements—plows (except for the share), carts, harrows, and many of the craftsman's tools—were made of wood, seasoned, split or rough-hewn. Few possessed saws; in Russia they were unknown before 1700. Iron was little used and was likely to be of poor quality. Though it might be less true of eastern Europe where, as in Bohemia, villages tended to be smaller, the community would usually have craftsmen—a smith or a carpenter, for example—to satisfy most needs. More intricate skills were provided by traveling tinkers.

The isolated villager might hear of the outside world from such men. Those living around the main routes would fare better and gather news, at least indirectly, from merchants, students, pilgrims, and government officials or, less reputably, from beggars, gypsies, or deserters (a numerous class in most states). He might buy broadsheets, almanacs, and romances, produced by enterprising printers at centres such as Troyes, to be hawked around wherever there were a few who could read. So were kept alive what became a later generation's fairy tales, along with the magic and astrology that they were not reluctant to believe. Inn and church provided the setting for business, gossip, and rumour. Official reports and requirements were posted and village affairs were conducted in the church. The innkeeper might benefit from the cash of wayfarers but like others who provided a service, he relied chiefly on the produce of his own land. Thus, the rural economy consisted of innumerable self-sufficient units incapable of generating adequate demand for the development of large-scale manufactures. Each cluster of communities was isolated within its own market economy, proud, and suspicious of outsiders. Even where circumstances fostered liberty, peasants were pitifully inadequate in finding original solutions to age-old problems but were well-versed in strategies of survival, for they could draw on stores of empirical wisdom. They feared change just as they feared the night for its unknown terrors. Their customs and attitudes were those of people who lived on the brink: more babies might be born but there would be no increase in the food supply.

# THE ECONOMIC ENVIRONMENT

The seeds were sown for an industrial economy in Europe before the Industrial Revolution occurred.

## INNOVATION AND DEVELOPMENT

In the age of Isaac Newton the frontiers of science were shifting fast, and there was widespread interest in experiment and demonstration, but one effect was to complete the separation of a distinctive intellectual elite: the more advanced the ideas, the more difficult their transmission and application. There was a movement of thought rather than a scientific movement, a culture of inquiry rather than of enterprise. Only in the long term was the one to lead to the other, through the growing belief that material progress was possible. Meanwhile, advances were piecemeal, usually the work of individuals, often having no connection with business. Missing was not only that association of interests that characterizes industrial society but also the educational ground: schools and universities were wedded to traditional courses. Typical inventors of the early industrial age were untutored craftsmen, such as Richard Arkwright, James Watt, or John Wilkinson. Between advances in technology there could be long delays.

Britain was the country that experienced the breakthrough to higher levels of production. The description "Industrial Revolution" is misleading if applied to the economy as a whole, but innovations in techniques and organization led to such growth in iron, woolens, and, above all, cotton textiles in the second half of the 18th century that Britain established a significant lead. It was sustained by massive investment and by the wars following the French Revolution, which shut the Continent off from developments that in Britain were stimulated by war. Factors involved in the unique experience of a country that contained only 1 in 20 of Europe's inhabitants expose certain contrasting features of the European economy. The accumulation of capital had been assisted by agricultural improvement, the acquisition of colonies, the operation of chartered companies (notably the East India Company), trade-oriented policies of governments (notably that of William Pitt during the Seven Years' War), and the development of colonial markets. There existed a relatively advanced financial system, based on the successful Bank of England (founded 1694), and interest rates were consistently lower than those of European rivals. This was particularly important in the financing of road and canal building, where large private investment was needed before profit was realized. Further advantages included plentiful coal and iron ore and swift-flowing streams in the hilly northwest where the moist climate was suited to cotton spinning. The labour force was supplemented by Irish immigrants. A society that cherished political and legal institutions characteristic of the ancien régime also exhibited a free and tolerant spirit, tending to value fortune as much as birth. Comparison with Britain's chief rival in the successive wars of 1740–48, 1756–63, and 1778–83 is strengthened by the consequences of those wars: for France the slide toward bankruptcy, for Britain a larger debt that could still be funded without difficulty.

Yet the French enjoyed an eightfold growth in colonial trade between 1714 and 1789, considerably larger than that of the British. The Dutch still had the financial strength, colonies, trading connections, and at least some of the entrepreneurial spirit that had characterized them in the 17th century. Enlightened statesmen such as the Marquês de Pombal in Portugal, Charles III of Spain, and Joseph II of Austria backed measures designed to promote agriculture and manufacturing. The question of why other countries lagged behind Britain leads to consideration of material and physical conditions, collective attitudes, and government policies. It should not distort the picture of Europe as a whole or obscure the changes that affected the demand for goods and the ability of manufacturers and traders to respond.

The mercantilist theory—which still appealed to a statesman like Frederick the Great, as it had to his great-grandfather—was grounded on the assumption that markets were limited: to increase trade, new markets had to be found. Mobility within society and increased spending by common folk, who were not expected to live luxuriously, were treated as symptoms of disorder. Mercantilists were concerned lest the state be stripped of its treasure and proper distinctions of status be undermined. The moral context is important: mercantilism belongs to the world of the city-state, the guilds, and the church; its ethical teaching is anchored in the medieval situation. By 1600 the doctrine that usury was sinful was already weakened beyond recovery by evasion and example. Needy princes borrowed, but prejudice against banks lingered, reinforced by periodic demonstrations of their fallibility, as in the failure of John Law's Banque Générale in Paris in 1720. Productive activity was not necessarily assumed to be a good thing. Yet it is possible, throughout the period, to identify dynamic features characteristic of capitalism in its developed, industrial phase.

## EARLY CAPITALISM

With more widespread adoption of utilitarian criteria for management went a sterner view of the obligation of workers. Respect for the clock, with regular hours and the reduction of holidays for saints' days (already achieved in Protestant countries), was preparing the way psychologically for the discipline of the factory and mill. Handsome streets and squares of merchants' houses witnessed to the prosperity of Atlantic ports such as Bordeaux, Nantes, and Bristol, which benefited from the reorientation of trade. Above all, Amsterdam and London reflected the mutually beneficial activity of trade and services. From shipbuilding, so demanding in skills and raw materials, a network of suppliers reached back to forests, fields, and forges, where timber, iron, canvas, and rope were first worked. Chandlering, insurance, brokerage, and credit-trading facilitated international

# MERCANTILISM

Mercantilism is an economic theory and practice common in Europe from the 16th to the 18th century that promoted governmental regulation of a nation's economy for the purpose of augmenting state power at the expense of rival national powers. It was the economic counterpart of political absolutism. Its 17th-century publicists—most notably Thomas Mun in England, Jean-Baptiste Colbert in France, and Antonio Serra in Italy—never, however, used the term themselves; it was given currency by the Scottish economist Adam Smith in his *Wealth of Nations* (1776).

Mercantilism contained many interlocking principles. Precious metals, such as gold and silver, were deemed indispensable to a nation's wealth. If a nation did not possess mines or have access to them, precious metals should be obtained by trade. It was believed that trade balances must be "favourable," meaning an excess of exports over imports. Colonial possessions should serve as markets for exports and as suppliers of raw materials to the mother country. Manufacturing was forbidden in colonies, and all commerce between colony and mother country was held to be a monopoly of the mother country.

A strong nation, according to the theory, was to have a large population, for a large population would provide a supply of labour, a market, and soldiers. Human wants were to be minimized, especially for imported luxury goods, for they drained off precious foreign exchange. Sumptuary laws (affecting food and drugs) were to be passed to make sure that wants were held low. Thrift, saving, and even parsimony were regarded as virtues, for only by these means could capital be created. In effect, mercantilism provided the favourable climate for the early development of capitalism, with its promises of profit.

Later, mercantilism was severely criticized. Advocates of laissez-faire argued that there was really no difference between

(*continued on the next page*)

**19**

## MERCANTILISM (CONTINUED)

domestic and foreign trade and that all trade was beneficial both to the trader and to the public. They also maintained that the amount of money or treasure that a state needed would be automatically adjusted and that money, like any other commodity, could exist in excess. They denied the idea that a nation could grow rich only at the expense of another and argued that trade was in reality a two-way street. Laissez-faire, like mercantilism, was challenged by other economic ideas.

dealing and amassing of capital. Fairs had long counteracted the isolation of regional economies: Lyon on the Rhône, Hamburg on the Elbe, and Danzig on the Vistula had become centres of exchange, where sales were facilitated by price lists, auctions, and specialization in certain commodities.

Retailing acquired a modern look with shops catering to those who could afford coffee from Brazil or tobacco from Virginia; unlike earlier retailing, the goods offered for sale were not the products of work carried out on the premises. The dissemination of news was another strand in the pattern. By 1753 the sale of newspapers exceeded seven million: the emphasis was on news, not opinion, and price lists were carried with the news that affected them. Seamen were assisted by the dredging of harbours and improved docks and by more accurate navigational instruments and charts, not to mention a marked increase in the number of lighthouses on or off the shores of Europe. The state also improved roads and made them safe for travelers; canals linked rivers to facilitate trade.

## THE OLD INDUSTRIAL ORDER

Operations of high finance represented the future of capitalist Europe. The economy as a whole was still closer in most respects to the Middle Ages. The typical unit of production, however, was the domestic enterprise, with apprentices and journeymen living with family and servants. The merchant played a vital part in the provision of capital. When metalworkers made knives or needles for a local market, they could remain their own masters. For a larger market, they had to rely on businessmen for fuel, ore, wages, and transport. In textiles the capital and marketing skills of the entrepreneur were essential to cottagers. This putting-out system spread as merchants saw the advantages of evading guild control. When the cotton industry was developed around Rouen and Barcelona, it was organized in the same way as woolen textiles. In the old industrial order, output could be increased only in proportion to the number of workers involved. In England the new order was evolving, and ranks of machines in barracklike mills were producing for a mass market. The need to produce economically could transform an industry, as in Brabant, where peasants moved into the weaving side of the linen trade and then established bleaching works that ruined traditionally dominant Haarlem. It also altered the social balance, as in electoral Saxony where, between 1550 and 1750, the proportion of peasants who made most of their living by industry rose from 5 to 30 percent of the

*BEFORE THE INDUSTRIAL REVOLUTION, MANY PEOPLE MANUFACTURED GOODS, SUCH AS TEXTILES, IN THEIR HOMES. THIS GAVE RISE TO THE TERM "COTTAGE INDUSTRY."*

population. With such change came the dependence on capital and the market that was to make the worker so vulnerable.

Inevitably the expansion of domestic manufactures brought problems of control, which were eventually resolved by concentration in factories and by technical advances large enough to justify investment in machinery. Starting with the Lombe brothers' silk mills, their exploitation of secrets acquired from Italy (1733), and John Kay's flying shuttle, British inventions set textile production on a dizzy path of growth. Abraham Darby's process of coke smelting was perhaps the most important single improvement, since it liberated the iron founder from dependence on charcoal. The shortage of timber, a source of anxiety everywhere except in Russia and Scandinavia, proved to be a stimulus to invention and progress. Technical development on the Continent was less remarkable. Improvement could be modest indeed. A miller could grind 37 pounds (17 kilograms) of flour each day in the 12th century; by 1700 it might have been 55 pounds. In some areas there were long intervals between theoretical advances and technological application. Galileo, Evangelista Torricelli, Otto von Guericke, and Blaise Pascal worked on the vacuum in the first half of the 17th century, and Denis Papin later experimented with steam engines; however, it was not until 1711 that Thomas Newcomen produced a model that was of any practical use despite the great need for power. Mining, already well advanced, was held back by difficulties of drainage. In the Rohrerbuhel copper mines in the Tyrol, the Heiliger Geist shaft, at 2,900 feet (886 metres), remained the deepest in the world until 1872; a third of its labour force was employed in draining. Increases in productivity were generally found in those manufacturing activities where, as in the part-time production of linen in Silesia, the skills required were modest and the raw material could be produced locally.

Specialized manufacturing, evolving to meet the rising demand generated by the enrichment of the upper classes, showed significant growth. Wherever technical ingenuity was challenged by the needs of the market, results could be impressive. Printing was of seminal importance, since the advance of knowledge depended on it. Improvements in type molds and founding contributed to a threefold increase between 1600 and 1700 in the number of pages printed in a day. The Hollander, a pulverizing machine (c. 1670), could produce more pulp for paper than eight stamping mills. The connection between technical innovation and style is illustrated by improvements in glassmaking that made possible not only the casting of large sheets for mirrors but also, by 1700, the larger panes required for the sash windows that were replacing the leaded panes of casements. Venice lost its dominant position in the manufacture of glass as rulers set up works to save expensive imports. A new product sometimes followed a single discovery, as when the Saxons Ehrenfried Walter von Tschirnhaus and Johann Friedrich Böttger successfully imitated Chinese hard paste and created the porcelain of Meissen. A way of life could be affected by one invention. The pendulum clock of the Dutch scientist Christiaan Huygens introduced an age of reliable timekeeping. Clocks were produced in great numbers, and Geneva's production of 5,000 timepieces a year was overtaken by 1680 by the clockmakers of both London and Paris. With groups of workers each responsible for a particular task, such as the making of wheels or the decoration of dials, specialization led to enhanced production, and in these elegant products of traditional craftsmanship the division of labour appeared.

# TECHNOLOGY IN THE ERA PRECEDING THE INDUSTRIAL REVOLUTION

The technological history of the Middle Ages was one of slow but substantial development. In the succeeding period the tempo of change increased markedly and was associated with profound social, political, religious, and intellectual upheavals in western Europe.

The emergence of the nation-state, the cleavage of the Christian church by the Protestant Reformation, the Renaissance and its accompanying scientific revolution, and the overseas expansion of European states all had interactions with developing technology. This expansion became possible after the advance in naval technology opened up the ocean routes to Western navigators. The conversion of voyages of discovery into imperialism and colonization was made possible by the new firepower. The combination of light, maneuverable ships with the firepower of iron cannon gave European adventurers a decisive advantage, enhanced by other technological assets.

The Reformation, not itself a factor of major significance to the history of technology, nevertheless had interactions with it; the capacity of the new printing presses to disseminate all points of view contributed to the religious upheavals, while the intellectual ferment provoked by the Reformation resulted in a rigorous assertion of the vocational character of work and thus stimulated industrial and commercial activity and technological innovation. It is an indication of the nature of this encouragement that so many of the inventors and scientists of the period were Calvinists, Puritans, and, in England, Dissenters.

# THE RENAISSANCE

The Renaissance had more obviously technological content than the Reformation. The concept of "renaissance" is elusive. Since the scholars of the Middle Ages had already achieved a very full recovery of the literary legacy of the ancient world, as a "rebirth" of knowledge the Renaissance marked rather a point of transition after which the posture of deference to the ancients began to be replaced by a consciously dynamic, progressive attitude. Even while they looked back to Classical models, Renaissance men looked for ways of improving upon them. This attitude is outstandingly represented in the genius of Leonardo da Vinci. As an artist of original perception he was recognized by his contemporaries, but some of his most novel work is recorded in his notebooks and was virtually unknown in his own time. This included ingenious designs

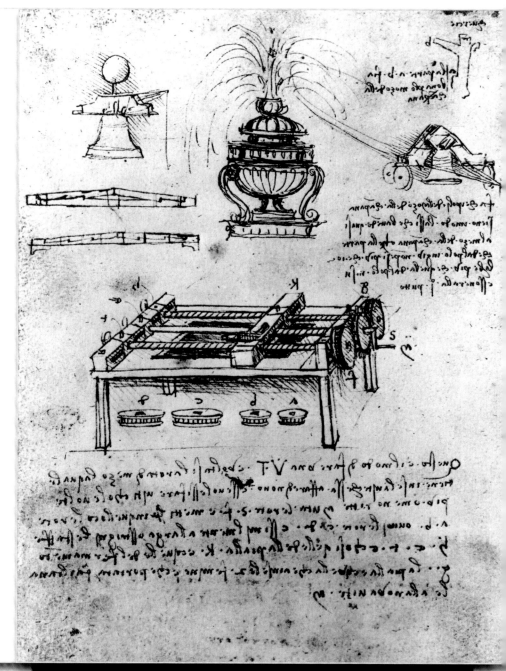

*SHOWN HERE ARE SKETCHES OF A SCREW-CUTTING MACHINE BY LEONARDO DA VINCI, C. 1500; IN THE BIBLIOTHÈQUE DE L'INSTITUT DE FRANCE, PARIS.*

for submarines, airplanes, and helicopters and drawings of elabourate trains of gears and of the patterns of flow in liquids. The early 16th century was not yet ready for these novelties: they met no specific social need, and the resources necessary for their development were not available.

An often overlooked aspect of the Renaissance is the scientific revolution that accompanied it. As with the term "Renaissance" itself, the concept is complex, having to do with intellectual liberation from the ancient world. For centuries the authority of Aristotle in dynamics, of Ptolemy in astronomy, and of Galen in medicine had been taken for granted. Beginning in the 16th century their authority was challenged and overthrown, and scientists set out by observation and experiment to establish new explanatory models of the natural world. One distinctive characteristic of these models was that they were tentative, never receiving the authoritarian prestige long accorded to the ancient masters. Since this fundamental shift of emphasis, science has been committed to a progressive, forward-looking attitude and has come increasingly to seek practical applications for scientific research.

Technology performed a service for science in this revolution by providing it with instruments that greatly enhanced its powers. The use of the telescope by Galileo to observe the moons of Jupiter was a dramatic example of this service, but the telescope was only one of many tools and instruments that proved valuable in navigation, mapmaking, and labouratory experiments. More significant were the services of the new sciences to technology, and the most important of these was the theoretical preparation for the invention of the steam engine.

# THE STEAM ENGINE

The researches of a number of scientists, especially those of Robert Boyle of England with atmospheric pressure, of Otto von Guericke of Germany with a vacuum, and of the French Huguenot Denis Papin with pressure vessels, helped to equip practical technologists with the theoretical basis of steam power. Distressingly little is known about the manner in which this knowledge was assimilated by pioneers such as Thomas Savery and Thomas Newcomen, but it is inconceivable that they could have been ignorant of it. Savery took out a patent for a "new Invention for Raiseing of Water and occasioning Motion to all Sorts of Mill Work by the Impellent Force of Fire" in 1698 (No. 356). His apparatus depended on the condensation of steam in a vessel, creating a partial vacuum into which water was forced by atmospheric pressure.

Credit for the first commercially successful steam engine, however, must go to Newcomen, who erected his first machine near Dudley Castle in Staffordshire in 1712. It operated by atmospheric pressure on the top face of a piston in a cylinder, in the lower part of which steam was condensed to create a partial vacuum. The piston was connected to one end of a rocking beam, the other end of which carried the pumping rod in the mine shaft. Newcomen was a tradesman in Dartmouth, Devon, and his engines were robust but unsophisticated. Their heavy fuel consumption made them uneconomical when used where coal was expensive, but in the British coalfields they performed an essential service by keeping deep mines clear of water and were extensively adopted for this purpose. In this way the early steam engines fulfilled one of the most pressing needs of British industry in the 18th century. Although waterpower and wind

*Shown here is a Newcomen steam engine, 1747.*

power remained the basic sources of power for industry, a new prime mover had thus appeared in the shape of the steam engine, with tremendous potential for further development as and when new applications could be found for it.

## THOMAS NEWCOMEN

Thomas Newcomen (1664–1729) was a British engineer and inventor of the atmospheric steam engine, a precursor of James Watt's engine. As an ironmonger at Dartmouth, Newcomen became aware of the high cost of using the power of horses to pump water out of the Cornish tin mines. With his assistant John Calley (or Cawley), a plumber, he experimented for more than 10 years with a steam pump. It was superior to the crude pump of Thomas Savery. In Newcomen's engine the intensity of pressure was not limited by the pressure of the steam. Instead, atmospheric pressure pushed the piston down after the condensation of steam had created a vacuum in the cylinder.

As Savery had obtained a broad patent for his pump in 1698, Newcomen could not patent his engine. Therefore, he entered into partnership with Savery. The first recorded Newcomen engine was erected near Dudley Castle, Staffordshire, in 1712.

Newcomen invented the internal-condensing jet for obtaining a vacuum in the cylinder and an automatic valve gear. By using steam at atmospheric pressure, he kept within the working limits of his materials. For a number of years, Newcomen's engine was used in the draining of mines and in raising water to power waterwheels.

# METALLURGY AND MINING

One cause of the rising demand for coal in Britain was the depletion of the woodland and supplies of charcoal, making manufacturers anxious to find a new source of fuel. Of particular importance were experiments of the iron industry in using coal instead of charcoal to smelt iron ore and to process cast iron into wrought iron and steel. The first success in these attempts came in 1709, when Abraham Darby, a Quaker ironfounder in Shropshire, used coke to reduce iron ore in his enlarged and improved blast furnace. Other processes, such as glassmaking, brickmaking, and the manufacture of pottery, had already adopted coal as their staple fuel. Great technical improvements had taken place in all these processes. In ceramics, for instance, the long efforts of European manufacturers to imitate the hard, translucent quality of Chinese porcelain culminated in Meissen at the beginning of the 18th century; the process was subsequently discovered independently in Britain in the middle of the century. Stoneware, requiring a lower firing temperature than porcelain, had achieved great decorative distinction in the 17th century as a result of the Dutch success with opaque white tin glazes at their Delft potteries, and the process had been widely imitated.

The period from 1500 to 1750 witnessed a steady expansion in mining for minerals other than coal and iron. The gold and silver mines of Saxony and Bohemia provided the inspiration for the treatise by Agricola, *De re metallica*, which distilled the cumulative experience of several centuries in mining and metalworking and became, with the help of some brilliant woodcuts and the printing press, a worldwide manual on mining practice. Queen Elizabeth I introduced German

*THIS ENGRAVING FROM* DE RE METALLICA (ON THE NATURE OF METALS), *BY GEORGIUS AGRICOLA (1494–1555), ALSO KNOWN AS GEORG PAWER, WAS PUBLISHED IN BASEL IN 1556.*

miners to England in order to develop the mineral resources of the country, and one result of this was the establishment of brass manufacture. This metal, an alloy of copper and zinc, had been known in the ancient world and in Eastern civilizations but was not developed commercially in western Europe until the 17th century. Metallic zinc had still not been isolated, but brass was made by heating copper with charcoal and calamine, an oxide of zinc mined in England in the Mendip Hills and elsewhere, and was worked up by hammering, annealing (a heating process to soften the material), and wiredrawing into a wide range of household and industrial commodities. Other nonferrous metals such as tin and lead were sought out and exploited with increasing enterprise in this period, but as their ores commonly occurred at some distance from sources of coal, as in the case of the Cornish tin mines, the employment of Newcomen engines to assist in drainage was rarely economical, and this circumstance restricted the extent of the mining operations.

## NEW COMMODITIES

Following the dramatic expansion of the European nations into the Indian Ocean region and the New World, the commodities of these parts of the world found their way back into Europe in increasing volume. These commodities created new social habits and fashions and called for new techniques of manufacture. Tea became an important trade commodity but was soon surpassed in volume and importance by the products of specially designed plantations, such as sugar, tobacco, cotton, and cocoa. Sugar refining, depending on the crystallization of sugar from the syrupy molasses derived from the cane, became an important industry. So did the processing of tobacco, for smoking in clay pipes (produced in bulk at Delft and elsewhere) or for taking as snuff. Cotton had been known before as an Eastern plant, but its successful transplantation to the New World made much greater quantities available and stimulated the emergence of an important new textile industry.

The woolen cloth industry in Britain provided a model and precedent upon which the new cotton industry could build. Already in the Middle Ages, the processes of cloth manufacture had been partially mechanized upon the introduction of fulling mills and the use of spinning wheels. But in the 18th century the industry remained almost entirely a domestic or cottage one, with most of the processing being performed in the homes of the workers, using comparatively simple tools that could be operated by hand or foot. The most complicated apparatus was the loom, but this could usually be worked by a single weaver, although wider cloths required an assistant. It was a general practice to install the loom in an upstairs room with a long window giving maximum natural light. Weaving was regarded as a man's work, spinning being assigned to the women of the family (hence, "spinsters"). The weaver could use the yarn provided by up to a dozen spinsters, and the balanced division of labour was preserved by the weaver's assuming responsibility for supervising the cloth through the other processes, such as fulling. Pressures to increase the productivity of various operations had already produced some technical innovations by the first half of the 18th century. The first attempts at devising a spinning machine, however, were not successful; and without this, John Kay's technically successful flying shuttle (a device for hitting the shuttle from one side of the loom to the other, dispensing with the need to pass it through by hand) did not fulfill an obvious need. It was not until the rapid

## JOHN KAY

John Kay (1704–c. 1780) was an English machinist and engineer. He was the inventor of the flying shuttle, which was an important step toward automatic weaving.

The son of a woolen manufacturer, Kay was placed in charge of his father's mill while still a youth. He made many improvements in dressing, batting, and carding machinery. On May 26, 1733, he received a patent for a "New Engine or Machine for Opening and Dressing Wool" that incorporated his flying shuttle. In previous looms, the shuttle was thrown, or passed, through the warp threads by hand, and wide fabrics required two weavers seated side by side passing the shuttle from left to right and then back again. Kay mounted his shuttle on wheels in a track and used paddles to shoot the shuttle from side to side when the weaver jerked a cord. Using the flying shuttle, one weaver could weave fabrics of any width more quickly than two could before.

Woolen manufacturers in Yorkshire were quick to adopt the new invention, but they organized a protective club to avoid paying Kay a royalty. After he lost most of his money in litigation to protect his patent, Kay moved to France, where he is said to have died in obscurity. Kay's invention so increased yarn consumption that it spurred the invention of spinning machines, but its true importance lay in its adaptation in power looms.

rise of the cotton cloth industry that the old, balanced industrial system was seriously upset and that a new, mechanized system, organized on the basis of factory production, began to emerge.

## AGRICULTURE

Another major area that began to show signs of profound change in the 18th century was agriculture. Stimulated by greater commercial activity, the rising market for food caused by an increasing population aspiring to a higher standard of living, and by the British aristocratic taste for improving estates to provide affluent and decorative country houses, the traditional agricultural system of Britain was transformed. It is important to note that this was a British development, as it is one of the indications of the increasing pressures of industrialization there even before the Industrial Revolution, while other European countries, with the exception of the Netherlands, from which several of the agricultural innovations in Britain were acquired, did little to encourage agricultural productivity. The nature of the transformation was complex, and it was not completed until well into the 19th century. It consisted partly of a legal reallocation of land ownership, the "enclosure" movement, to make farms more compact and economical to operate. In part also it was brought about by the increased investment in farming improvements because the landowners felt encouraged to invest money in their estates instead of merely drawing rents from them. Again, it consisted of using this money for technical improvements, taking the form of machinery—such as Jethro Tull's mechanical sower—of better drainage, of scientific methods of breeding to raise the quality of livestock, and of experimenting with new crops and systems of crop rotation. The process has often been described as an agricultural revolution, but it is preferable to regard it as an essential prelude to and part of the Industrial Revolution.

*Jethro Tull was a major figure of the British agricultural revolution. Among his innovations were a horse-drawn seed drill and a horse-drawn hoe.*

## CONSTRUCTION

Construction techniques did not undergo any great change in the period 1500–1750. The practice of building in stone and brick became general, although timber remained an important building material for roofs and floors, and, in areas in which stone was in short supply, the half-timber type of construction retained its popularity into the 17th century. Thereafter, however, the spread of brick and tile manufacturing provided a cheap and readily available substitute, although it suffered an eclipse on aesthetic grounds in the 18th century, when Classical styles enjoyed a vogue and brick came to be regarded as inappropriate for facing such buildings. Brickmaking, however, had become an important industry for ordinary domestic building by then and, indeed, entered into the export trade as Dutch and Swedish ships regularly carried brick as ballast to the New World, providing a valuable building material for the early American settlements. Cast iron was coming into use in buildings, but only for decorative purposes. Glass was also beginning to become an important feature of buildings of all sorts, encouraging the development of an industry that still relied largely on ancient skills of fusing sand to make glass and blowing, molding, and cutting it into the shapes required.

More substantial constructional techniques were required in land drainage and military fortification, although again their importance is shown rather in their scale and complexity than in any novel features. The Dutch, wrestling with the sea for centuries, had devised extensive dikes; their techniques were borrowed by English landowners in the 17th century in an attempt to reclaim tracts of fenlands.

In military fortification, the French strongholds designed by Sébastien de Vauban in the late 17th century demonstrated how warfare had adapted to the new weapons and, in particular, to heavy artillery. With earthen embankments to protect their salients, these star-shaped fortresses were virtually impregnable to the assault weapons of the day. Firearms remained cumbersome, with awkward firing devices and slow reloading. The quality of weapons improved somewhat as gunsmiths became more skillful.

# TRANSPORT AND COMMUNICATIONS

Like constructional techniques, transport and communications made substantial progress without any great technical innovations. Road building was greatly improved in France, and, with the completion of the Canal du Midi between the Mediterranean and the Bay of Biscay in 1692, large-scale civil engineering achieved an outstanding success. The canal is 150 miles (241 km) long, with a hundred locks, a tunnel, three major aqueducts, many culverts, and a large summit reservoir.

The sea remained the greatest highway of commerce, stimulating innovation in the sailing ship. The Elizabethan galleon with its great maneuverability and firepower, the Dutch herring busses and fluitschips with their commodious hulls and shallow draft, the versatile East Indiamen of both the Dutch and the British East India companies, and the mighty ships of the line produced for the French and British navies in the 18th century indicate some of the main directions of evolution.

The needs of reliable navigation created a demand for better instruments. The quadrant was improved by conversion

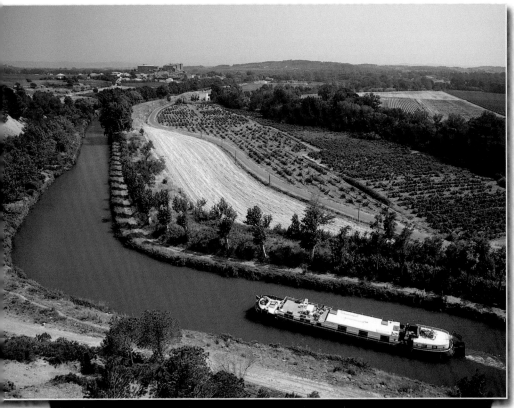

*A BARGE FLOATS ON THE MIDI CANAL (CANAL DU MIDI), IN THE LANGUEDOC REGION OF FRANCE.*

to the octant, using mirrors to align the image of a star with the horizon and to measure its angle more accurately: with further refinements the modern sextant evolved. Even more significant was the ingenuity shown by scientists and instrument makers in the construction of a clock that would keep accurate time at sea: such a clock, by showing the time in Greenwich when it was noon aboard ship would show how far east or west of Greenwich the ship lay (longitude). A prize of £20,000 was offered by the British Board of Longitude for this purpose in 1714, but it was not awarded until 1763 when

**41**

John Harrison's so-called No. 4 chronometer fulfilled all the requirements.

# CHEMISTRY

Robert Boyle's contribution to the theory of steam power has been mentioned, but Boyle is more commonly recognized as the "father of chemistry," in which field he was responsible for the recognition of an element as a material that cannot be resolved into other substances. It was not until the end of the 18th and the beginning of the 19th century, however, that the work of Antoine Lavoisier and John Dalton put modern chemical science on a firm theoretical basis. Chemistry was still struggling to free itself from the traditions of alchemy. Even alchemy was not without practical applications, for it promoted experiments with materials and led to the development of specialized labouratory equipment that was used in the manufacture of dyes, cosmetics, and certain pharmaceutical products. For the most part, pharmacy still relied upon recipes based on herbs and other natural products, but the systematic preparation of these eventually led to the discovery of useful new drugs.

The period from 1500 to 1750 witnessed the emergence of Western technology in the sense that the superior techniques of Western civilization enabled the nations that composed it to expand their influence over the whole known world. Yet, with the exception of the steam engine, this period was not marked by outstanding technological innovation. What was, perhaps, more important than any particular innovation was the evolution, however faltering and partial and limited to Britain in the first place, of a technique of innovation, or what has been called "the

## CANAL DU MIDI

Located in the Languedoc region of France, the Canal du Midi is a major link in the inland waterway system from the Atlantic Ocean to the Mediterranean Sea. It was built in the 17th century at a time when France was the centre of civil engineering excellence. Louis XIV granted permission for the construction of the canal in 1666 to designer Pierre-Paul, Baron Riquet de Bonrepos. Work was soon under way on the water supply system, the most difficult part being construction of the Saint-Ferréol Dam. It is 780 metres (2,560 feet) in length and 32 metres (105 feet) in height, and it holds 6,374,000 cubic metres (about 1,402,100,000 gallons) of water. At the time, it was the greatest civil engineering work in Europe, holding back waters from the Montagne Noire, including the Laudot River, which could feed either the canal or the reservoir via two channels with a total length of 66 km (41 miles).

Despite political and financial pressure, Riquet pushed ahead with construction of the canal, though it affected his health. He died eight months before his canal opened in May 1681. In addition to some 100 locks, the project required building numerous bridges, an aqueduct, and the world's first canal tunnel. The Malpas Tunnel was 165 metres (541 feet) long and 7.4 metres (24 feet) wide, and it was 5.85 metres (19 feet) above water level; for some reason, it was built to much more generous proportions than any of the canal's bridges. There were many problems during construction. One lock collapsed in 1670, and Riquet had to redesign and rebuild those already constructed. The canal also had to pass a steep rocky slope at Pechlaurier, and there gunpowder was used—perhaps the first use of explosives for civil engineering. At one time 12,000 people were working under Riquet's command, the labour force being split into 12 divisions so that control could be maintained.

(*continued on the next page*)

## CANAL DU MIDI (CONTINUED)

Following Riquet's death, his sons, together with the celebrated French engineer Sébastien Le Prestre de Vauban, continued work on improving the canal. By 1692 these improvements had been completed, and travelers from around the world came to examine the canal. Although it was fairly successful financially, the canal never carried ships from the Atlantic to the Mediterranean. Until the Canal de Beaucaire opened from Sète to the Rhône in 1808, the Canal du Midi was isolated from the rest of France's canal system. However, it was Europe's first long-distance canal and was designated a UNESCO World Heritage site in 1996.

invention of invention." The creation of a political and social environment conducive to invention, the building up of vast commercial resources to support inventions likely to produce profitable results, the exploitation of mineral, agricultural, and other raw material resources for industrial purposes, and, above all, the recognition of specific needs for invention and an unwillingness to be defeated by difficulties, together produced a society ripe for an industrial revolution based on technological innovation. The technological achievements of the period 1500–1750, therefore, must be judged in part by their substantial contribution to the spectacular innovations of the following period.

## CHAPTER 3

# THE INDUSTRIAL REVOLUTION BEGINS IN ENGLAND

Most products people in the industrialized nations use today are turned out swiftly by the process of mass production, by people (and sometimes by robots) working on assembly lines using power-driven machines. As has been discussed, people of ancient and medieval times had no such products. They had to spend long, tedious hours of hand labour even on simple objects. The energy, or power, they employed in work came almost wholly from their own and their animals' muscles. Thanks to the Industrial Revolution, machines changed people's way of life as well as their methods of manufacture.

About the time of the American Revolution, the people of England began to use machines to make cloth and steam engines to run the machines. A little later they invented locomotives. Productivity began a spectacular climb. By 1850 most Englishmen were labouring in industrial towns and Great Britain had become the workshop of the world. From Britain the Industrial Revolution spread gradually throughout Europe and to the United States.

# CHANGES THAT LED TO THE REVOLUTION

The most important of the changes that brought about the Industrial Revolution were (1) the invention of machines to do the work of hand tools; (2) the use of steam, and later of other kinds of power, in place of the muscles of human beings and of animals; and (3) the adoption of the factory system.

The Industrial Revolution came gradually. It happened in a short span of time, however, when measured against the centuries people had worked entirely by hand. Until John Kay invented the flying shuttle for looms in 1733 and James Hargreaves the spinning jenny 31 years later, the making of yarn and the weaving of cloth had been much the same for thousands of years. By 1800 a host of new and faster processes were in use in both manufacture and transportation.

This relatively sudden change in the way people lived deserves to be called a revolution. It differs from a political revolution in its greater effects on the lives of people and in not coming to an end, as, for example, did the French Revolution.

Instead, the Industrial Revolution grew more powerful each year as new inventions and manufacturing processes added to the efficiency of machines and increased productivity. Indeed, since World War I the mechanization of industry increased so enormously that another revolution in production has taken place.

# EXPANDING COMMERCE AFFECTS INDUSTRY

Commerce and industry have always been closely related. Sometimes one is ahead and sometimes the other, but the one behind is always trying to catch up. Beginning about 1400, world commerce grew and changed so greatly that writers sometimes use the term "commercial revolution" to describe the economic progress of the next three and a half centuries.

Many factors helped bring about this revolution in trade. The Crusades opened up the riches of the East to western Europe. America was discovered, and European nations began to acquire rich colonies there and elsewhere. New trade routes were opened. The strong central governments that replaced the feudal system began to protect and help their merchants. Trading firms, such as the British East India Company, were chartered by governments. Larger ships were built, and flourishing cities grew up.

With the expansion of trade, more money was needed. Large-scale commerce could not be carried on by barter, as much of the earlier trade had been. Gold and silver from the New World helped meet this need. Banks and credit systems developed. By the end of the 17th century Europe had a large accumulation of capital. Money had to be available before machinery and steam engines could come into wide use for they were costly to manufacture and install.

By 1750 large quantities of goods were being exchanged among the European nations, and there was a demand for more goods than were being produced. England was the leading commercial nation, and the manufacture of cloth was its leading industry.

## ORGANIZING PRODUCTION

Several systems of making goods had grown up by the time of the Industrial Revolution. In country districts families produced most of the food, clothing, and other articles they used, as they had done for centuries. In the cities merchandise was made in shops much like those of the medieval craftsmen, and manufacturing was strictly regulated by the guilds and by the government. The goods made in these shops, though of high quality, were limited and costly.

The merchants needed cheaper items, as well as larger quantities, for their growing trade. As early as the 15th century they already had begun to go outside the cities, beyond the reach of the hampering regulations, and to establish another system of producing goods.

## FROM COTTAGE INDUSTRY TO FACTORY

Cloth merchants, for instance, would buy raw wool from the sheep owners, have it spun into yarn by farmers' wives, and take it to country weavers to be made into textiles. These country weavers could manufacture the cloth more cheaply than city craftsmen could because they got part of their living from their gardens or small farms.

The merchants would then collect the cloth and give it out again to finishers and dyers. Thus, they controlled cloth making from start to finish. Similar methods of organizing and controlling the process of manufacture came to prevail in other industries, such as the nail, cutlery, and leather goods industries.

Some writers call this the putting-out system. Others call it the domestic system because the work was done in the home

*CLOTHING AND OTHER ITEMS WERE MANUFACTURED IN CITY SHOPS. THESE GOODS WERE COSTLY BECAUSE THEY WERE HANDMADE.*

("domestic" comes from the Latin word for home). Another term is "cottage industry," for most of the workers belonged to the class of farm labourers known as cotters and carried on the work in their cottages.

This system of industry had several advantages over older systems. It gave the merchant a large supply of manufactured articles at a low price. It also enabled him to order the particular kinds of items that he needed for his markets. It provided employment for every member of a craft worker's family and gave jobs to skilled workers who had no capital to start businesses for themselves. A few merchants who had enough capital had gone a step further. They brought workers together under one roof and supplied them with spinning wheels and looms or with the implements of other trades. These establishments were factories, though they bear slight resemblance to the factories of today.

## WHY THE REVOLUTION BEGAN IN ENGLAND

English merchants were leaders in developing a commerce that increased the demand for more goods. The expansion in trade had made it possible to accumulate capital to use in industry. A cheaper system of production had grown up that was largely free from regulation.

There also were new ideas in England that aided the movement. One of these was the growing interest in scientific investigation and invention. Another was the doctrine of laissez-faire, or letting business alone. This doctrine had been growing in favour throughout the 18th century. It was especially popular after the British economist Adam Smith argued powerfully for it in his great work *The Wealth of Nations* (1776).

For centuries the craft guilds and the government had controlled commerce and industry down to the smallest detail. Now many Englishmen had come to believe that it was better to let business be regulated by the free play of supply and demand rather than by laws. Thus, the English government for the most part kept its hands off and left business free to adopt the new inventions and the methods of production that were best suited to them.

The most important of the machines that ushered in the Industrial Revolution were invented in the last third of the 18th century. Earlier in the century, however, three inventions had been made that opened the way for the later machines. One was the crude, slow-moving steam engine built by Thomas Newcomen (1705), which was used to pump water out of mines. The second was Kay's flying shuttle (1733). It enabled one person to handle a wide loom more rapidly than two persons could operate it before. The third was a frame for spinning cotton thread with rollers, first set up by Lewis Paul and John Wyatt (1741). Their invention was not commercially practical, but it was the first step toward solving the problem of machine spinning.

# INVENTIONS IN TEXTILE INDUSTRY

As the flying shuttle sped up weaving, the demand for cotton yarn increased. Many inventors set to work to improve the spinning wheel. James Hargreaves, a weaver who was also a carpenter, patented his spinning jenny in 1770. It enabled one worker to run eight spindles instead of one.

About the same time Richard Arkwright developed his water frame, a machine for spinning with rollers operated by water power. In 1779 Samuel Crompton, a spinner, combined Hargreaves's jenny and Arkwright's roller frame into a spinning machine, called a mule. It produced thread of greater fineness and strength than the jenny or the roller frame. Since the roller frame and the mule were large and heavy, it became the practice to install them in mills, where they could be run by water power. They were tended by women and children.

These improvements in spinning machinery called for further improvements in weaving. In 1785 Edmund Cartwright

*THE SPINNING JENNY WAS USED FOR SPINNING WOOL AND COTTON.*

patented a power loom. In spite of the need for it, weaving machinery came into use very slowly. First, many improvements had to be made before the loom was satisfactory. Second, the hand weavers violently opposed its adoption because it threw many of them out of work. Those who got jobs in the factories were obliged to take the same pay as unskilled workers. Thus, some people rioted, smashed the machines, and tried to prevent their use. The power loom was only coming into wide operation in the cotton industry by 1813. It did not completely replace the hand loom in weaving cotton until 1850. It was not well adapted to the making of some woolens. As late as 1880 many hand looms were still in use for weaving woolen cloth.

Many other machines contributed to the progress of the textile industry. In 1785 Thomas Bell of Glasgow, Scotland, invented cylinder printing of cotton goods. This was a great improvement on block printing. It made successive impressions of a design "join up" and did the work more rapidly and more cheaply. In 1793 the available supply of cotton was increased by American Eli Whitney's invention of the cotton gin. In 1804 J.M. Jacquard, a Frenchman, perfected a loom on which patterns might be woven in fabrics by mechanical means. This loom was later adapted to the making of lace, which became available to everyone.

## WATT'S STEAM ENGINE

While textile machinery was developing, progress was being made in other directions. In 1763 James Watt, a Scottish mechanic, was asked to repair a model of a Newcomen steam engine. He saw how crude and inefficient it was and by a series of improvements made it a practical device for running machinery.

Wheels turned by running water had been the chief source of power for the early factories. These were necessarily situated on swift-running streams. When the steam engine became efficient, it was possible to locate factories in more convenient places.

## COAL AND IRON

The first users of steam engines were the coal and iron industries. They were destined to be basic industries in the new age of

THIS ARTIST'S DEPICTION SHOWS JAMES WATT INVENTING THE SEPARATE CONDENSER FOR THE STEAM ENGINE.

# JAMES WATT

It is sometimes said that James Watt got the idea for a steam engine while still a boy, watching steam lift the lid of his mother's teakettle. The truth is that Watt did not invent the steam engine; however, he made major improvements on the inefficient steam engine of his time.

James Watt was born in Greenock, Scotland, on Jan. 19, 1736. His father ran a successful ship- and house-building business. He apprenticed to an instrument maker in London in 1755. In 1767 he became instrument maker for the University of Glasgow, where he developed his lifelong interest in steam engines. For more than a century, inventors had tried to use steam power for pumping water from England's coal mines. The best result in Watt's time was an inefficient engine patented in 1705 by Thomas Newcomen, John Cawley, and Thomas Savery.

Watt was given the opportunity to improve on this slow and wasteful engine when the university's model needed repair in 1764. One improvement gained speed by making the engine double-acting. Watt did this with valves that admitted steam to each side of the piston in turn. At each admission to one side, the valves released the steam on the other side to a separate vessel, where it was condensed. This avoided chilling the cylinder at each stroke, and the condensation created a vacuum that made the new steam more effective. Watt obtained his first patent in 1769.

Watt's engine was very successful in pumping. For turning wheels in factories, however, it needed some device for changing the back-and-forth motion of the piston into rotary motion. So Watt made the piston drive a connecting rod and a crank that turned an axle. A former employee patented the crank, and Watt had to use less adequate methods for securing circular motion until the patent expired in 1781.

Watt immigrated to Birmingham, England, in 1774. There he won

(*continued on the next page*)

## JAMES WATT (CONTINUED)

the support of the manufacturer Matthew Boulton, and in 1775 the two men formed a partnership that would last 25 years. The financial support that Boulton was able to provide made possible rapid progress with the engine.

Watt never developed engines that were powerful for their weight, because he refused to use high-pressure steam. Another improvement, however, was his steam governor. The governor used two heavy balls, mounted on swinging arms. The arms were connected to regulate the steam valve. The whole assembly was geared to rotate with the engine's motion. It also maintained the motion at a desired speed. If the engine sped up, centrifugal force drove the balls outward in wider circles. This moved the arms. The arms choked the steam valve, thereby reducing speed. If the engine lagged, the balls lowered and admitted more steam. By 1790 Watt had earned enough money to let him retire to his estate near Birmingham, where he died on Aug. 25, 1819.

machinery. As early as 1720 many steam engines were in operation. In coal mines they pumped out the water that usually flooded the deep shafts. In the iron industry they pumped water to create the draft in blast furnaces.

The iron industry benefited also from other early inventions of the 18th century. Iron was scarce and costly, and production was falling off because England's forests could not supply enough charcoal for smelting the ore. Ironmasters had long been experimenting with coal as a fuel for smelting. Finally the Darby family, after three generations of effort, succeeded with coal that had been transformed into coke. This created a new demand for coal and laid the foundation for the British coal industry. The next great steps were taken in the 1780s, when Henry Cort developed the processes of puddling and rolling. Puddling produced nearly pure malleable iron. Hand in hand with the adoption of the new inventions went the rapid development of the factory system of manufacture.

## CHANGING CONDITIONS IN ENGLAND

The new methods increased the amount of goods produced and decreased the cost. The worker at a machine with 100 spindles on it could spin 100 threads of cotton more rapidly than 100 workers could on the old spinning wheels. Southern planters in the United States were able to meet the increased demand for raw cotton because they were using the cotton gin. This machine could do the job of 50 men in cleaning cotton. Similar improvements were being made in other lines of industry. British merchants no longer found it a problem to obtain enough goods to supply their markets. On the contrary, at times the markets were glutted with more goods than could be sold. Then mills were closed and workers were thrown out of employment.

With English factories calling for supplies, such as American cotton, and sending goods to all parts of the world, better transportation was needed. The roads of England were wretchedly poor and often impassable. Packhorses and wagons crawled along them, carrying small loads. Such slow and inadequate transportation kept the cost of goods high. Here again the need produced the invention. Thomas Telford and John McAdam each developed a method of road construction better than any that had been known since the ancient Romans built their famous roads.

## BUILDING CANALS AND RAILWAYS

Many canals were dug. They connected the main rivers and so furnished a network of waterways for transporting coal and other heavy goods. A canalboat held much more than a wagon. It moved smoothly if slowly over the water, with a single horse hitched to the towline. In some places, where it was impossible to dig canals and where heavy loads of coal had to be hauled, mine owners laid down wooden or iron rails. On these early railroads one horse could haul as much coal as 20 horses could on ordinary roads.

Early in the 19th century came George Stephenson's locomotive and Robert Fulton's steamboat, an American invention. These inventions marked the beginning of modern transportation on land and sea. Railroads called for the production of more goods, for they put factory-made products within reach of many more people at prices they could afford to pay.

## URBANIZATION AND CHANGES IN RURAL LIFE

As conditions in industry changed, social and political conditions changed with them. Farm labourers and artisans flocked to the manufacturing centers and became industrial workers. Cities grew rapidly. Factory centers such as Manchester, England, grew from villages into cities of hundreds of thousands in a few short decades. The percentage of the total population located in cities expanded steadily, and big cities tended to displace more scattered centers in western Europe's urban map. Rapid city growth produced new hardships, for housing stock

*THE ERIE CANAL, CONNECTING THE HUDSON VALLEY WITH THE GREAT LAKES, WAS COMPLETED IN 1825 AT A COST OF $7 MILLION. IT IMMEDIATELY BROUGHT ECONOMIC GAINS TO NEW YORK AND STIMULATED DEVELOPMENT ALONG ITS ENTIRE ROUTE.*

and sanitary facilities could not keep pace, though innovation slowly responded. Gas lighting improved street conditions in the better city neighborhoods from the 1830s onward, and sanitary reformers pressed for underground sewage systems at about this time. For those who were better-off, rapid suburban growth allowed some escape from the worst urban miseries.

Rural life also changed. As cities grew, the percentage of farmers in the total population declined. Although a full-scale technological revolution in the countryside occurred only after the 1850s, factory-made tools spread widely even before this time.

## ROBERT FULTON

Robert Fulton was born on Nov. 14, 1765, on a Pennsylvania farm in what is now Fulton Township. At 17 he went to Philadelphia to work for a jeweler and to study art. He used his talents so well that at 21 he had $400 to invest in a farm for his widowed mother and sisters. He then went to London to study art with the well-known painter Benjamin West.

In England he made friends in the scientific and engineering fields. Soon his interest in art was forgotten in the midst of his work on a series of inventions, including dredging machines, flax-spinning and rope-making devices, and a substitute for canal locks.

In 1797 he proposed the building of a submarine to the French government. It rejected his idea, but Fulton eventually built and launched *Nautilus* on his own in 1800. In Paris in 1801 he met the American minister Robert R. Livingston, who had obtained a 20-year monopoly on steamboat navigation in the state of New York. He returned to the United States as Livingston's partner to work out a practical steamboat, using an engine and boiler purchased in England from Boulton & Watt. On Aug. 17, 1807, Fulton's first steamboat, the *Clermont*, made a trial voyage—from New York Harbor, up the Hudson River, to Albany and back. The experiment was a triumph, discrediting skeptics who had called it "Fulton's folly." During the next eight years Fulton established and managed steamboat lines, and in 1814 he was commissioned by the federal government to build its first steam warship. He died in New York City on Feb. 24, 1815.

Scythes replaced sickles for harvesting, allowing a substantial improvement in productivity. Larger estates began to introduce newer equipment, such as grain drills for planting. Crop rotation, involving the use of nitrogen-fixing plants, displaced the age-old practice of leaving some land fallow, while better seeds and livestock and—from the 1830s—chemical fertilizers improved crop yields as well. Rising agricultural production and market specialization were central to the growth of cities and factories.

# THE CONDITION OF LABOUR

Far-reaching changes were gradually brought about in the life of industrial workers. For one thing, machines took a great burden of physical work from the muscles of human beings. Some of the other changes, however, were not so welcome.

The change from domestic industry to the factory system meant a loss of independence to the worker. Home labourers could work whenever they pleased. Although the need for money often drove them to toil long hours at home, they could vary the monotony of the task by digging or planting a garden patch. When they became factory employees, however, they not only had to work long hours but had to leave the farm. Workers lived near the factory, often in a crowded slum district, and were forced to work continuously at the pace set by the machine. The long hours and the monotonous toil were an especially great hardship for the women and children. The vast majority of the jobs were held by them by 1816.

The change to industrialization was particularly hard on the weavers and the other skilled workers who sank to the position of factory workers. They had been independent masters—capitalists in a small way—and managers of their own businesses. They had pride in their skills. When they

saw themselves being forced into factories to do other men's bidding for the same pay as unskilled workers, it is no wonder that they rioted and broke up looms.

# PROBLEMS OF CAPITAL AND LABOUR

A person had to have a lot of capital to buy machines and open a factory. Those who were successful made huge profits with which to buy more machines, put up larger buildings, and purchase supplies in greater quantities at enormous savings. Thus, capital increased far more rapidly than it ever had before. Much of it was invested in building canals, railroads, and steamships and in developing foreign trade. The men who controlled these enterprises formed a powerful new class in England—the industrial capitalists.

The capitalists had a struggle to obtain a voice in the government. They needed a better system of banking, currency, and credit. They had to find and hold markets for their products. They had many difficulties in organizing their factories to run efficiently. They also had to make a profit on their investments in the face of intense competition.

Laissez-faire was the rule in England. This meant that the government had accepted the doctrine that it should keep hands off business. Factory owners could therefore arrange working conditions in whatever way they pleased. Grave problems arose for the workers—problems of long working

*IN THE ABSENCE OF GOVERNMENT REGULATIONS ON BUSINESSES, LABOURERS OFTEN TOILED IN HORRID CONDITIONS.*

hours, low wages, unemployment, accidents, employment of women and children, and poor housing conditions.

## IMPACT ON CHILDREN

The rapid development of large-scale manufacturing, especially during the early years of the Industrial Revolution, made possible the exploitation of young children in many factories. In England, as well as in other countries, there existed considerable demand for child labour during the 1800s. Children could tend many of the machines as well as older persons could, and they could be hired for less pay. Great numbers of children were worked from 12 to 14 hours a day under terrible conditions. Many were apprenticed to the factory owners and housed in miserable dormitories. Ill-fed and ill-clothed, they were sometimes driven under the lash of an overseer.

The high death rate of these child slaves eventually roused efforts to pass laws limiting the daily toil for apprentices. The first law, in 1802, which was aimed at controlling the apprenticeship of poor children to cotton-mill owners, was ineffective because it did not provide for enforcement. Several decades later, stronger reform laws began to emerge. Legislation in England, France, and Prussia during the 1830s, for instance, restricted the employment of young children in the factories and encouraged school attendance.

# CLASS DIVISIONS AND PROTEST MOVEMENTS

Along with the dramatic economic changes of the period, new antagonisms emerged among the urban social classes of England and other European countries. The key division lay between the members of the middle class, who owned businesses or acquired professional education, and those of the working class, who depended on the sale of their labour for a wage. Neither group was homogeneous. Many middle-class

# CHILD LABOUR

During the Industrial Revolution, children in the cities of Great Britain and other countries, including the United States, were forced to work in factories and shops in harsh conditions to help themselves and their families to survive. Outside cities, some children were put to work in mines. Children were paid very little and were made to work in cramped conditions, sometimes at precise work for which their small hands and keen eyesight were special assets.

At the beginning of the 19th century poor children—some only four years old—had workdays as long as 16 hours. At that time children made up about one-fourth of the total workforce of cotton mills in some regions of Great Britain. In one region, local government officials sent children from orphanages to the mills so that the government could be spared the cost of caring for them. In 1824 the father of the novelist Charles Dickens was sent to debtors' prison, and young Dickens, at age 12, had to work in a factory. Dickens later documented the harsh lives of poor children in such novels as *Oliver Twist* (published 1838).

The earliest efforts of the British government to curb child labour were unsuccessful. The first law that was effective, the Factory Act of 1833, forbade the employment of children under the age of 9. It also limited the number of hours older children could work: between ages 9 and 13 the limit was nine hours per day; between ages 13 and 18 the limit was 12 hours. The law also provided for state inspections. However, the Factory Act applied only to the textile industry and exempted many other industries, such as shipbuilding and the mining of iron and coal. In 1847 the workday of children between ages 13 and 18 was limited to 10 hours. Further legislation extended the regulations to other industries. In 1870 the introduction of compulsory education in Great Britain helped reduce the scale of child labour in the country.

(*continued on the next page*)

## CHILD LABOUR (CONTINUED)

Child labour was common in the United States from colonial times. The 1900 census showed that about 2 million children were employed. Many were engaged in mining and manufacturing. Roughly one in four workers in southern cotton mills were below age 15, and many were below age 12.

In 1904 a reform group called the National Child Labour Committee was organized, but it took a state-by-state approach to legal reform that proved to be inadequate. After at least one false start, the U.S. Congress in 1916 passed the Keating-Owens Child Labour Act, banning the sale of products from businesses that employed child workers under a specified age (which varied by type of industry) or that employed children under age 16 for more than eight hours per day. This law and another child labour law passed in 1918 were struck down by the U.S. Supreme Court, but support for reform grew. In the mid-1920s Congress passed a constitutional amendment that overruled the Supreme Court. Before the amendment had been ratified by enough states to take effect, the Fair Labour Standards Act of 1938 was passed. This law set a minimum age of 14 for employment outside school hours in nonmanufacturing jobs, of 16 for employment during school hours in interstate commerce, and of 18 for hazardous occupations. This law was upheld by the Supreme Court. Now, 14- and 15-year-olds are allowed to work under strict conditions (for no more than three hours on a school day or eight hours on a non-school day) and 16-year-olds are allowed to work on most non-farm jobs.

people criticized the profit-seeking behavior of the new factory owners. Some skilled workers, earning good wages, emulated middle-class people, seeking education and acquiring domestic trappings such as pianos.

*SOME CHILDREN OUTSIDE CITIES WERE PUT TO WORK IN MINES, WHERE THEY WERE USED FOR CHEAP AND SPECIALIZED LABOUR.*

Nevertheless, the social divide was considerable. It increasingly affected residential patterns, as wealthier classes moved away from the crowded slums of the poor, in contrast to the greater mixture in the quarters of preindustrial cities. City governments often enacted harsh measures against beggars, while new national laws attempted to make charity harder to obtain. The British Poor Law Reform of 1834, in particular, tightened the limits on relief in hopes of forcing able-bodied workers to fend for themselves.

Class divisions manifested themselves in protest movements. Middle-class people joined political protests hoping to win new rights against aristocratic monopoly. Workers increasingly organized on their own. Some workers attacked the reliance on machinery in the name of older, more humane traditions of work. Others formed incipient labour unions. These unions often started as "friendly societies" that collected dues from workers and extended aid during illness or unemployment. Soon, however, they became organizations for winning improvements by collective bargaining and strikes.

Industrial workers also sought to benefit themselves by political action. They fought such legislation as the English laws of 1799 and 1800 forbidding labour organizations. They campaigned to secure laws that would help them. National union movements arose in England during the 1820s, though they ultimately failed. Huge strikes in the silk industry around Lyon, France, in 1831 and 1834 sought a living minimum wage for all workers. The most ambitious worker movements tended to emphasize a desire to turn back the clock to older work systems where there was greater equality and a greater commitment to craft skill, but most failed. Smaller, local unions did achieve some success in preserving the conditions of traditional systems. The struggle by workers to extend their political power was one of the major factors in the spread of democracy during the 19th century.

# REVOLUTION SPREADS TO THE UNITED STATES

Until 1815 France was busy with the Napoleonic Wars. It had little opportunity to introduce machinery. When peace came France began to follow England. It followed slowly, however, and has never devoted itself as exclusively to manufacturing as England has. Belgium was ahead of France in adopting the new methods. The other European countries made little progress until the second half of the 19th century.

The United States too was slow in adopting machine methods of manufacture. Farming and trading were its chief interests until the Civil War. The new nation had little capital with which to buy the machinery and put up the buildings required. Such capital as existed was largely invested in shipping and commerce. Labour was scarce because men continued to push westward, clearing the forests and establishing themselves on the land.

A start in manufacturing, however, was made in New England in 1790 by Samuel Slater. An employee of Arkwright's spinning mills, Slater came to the United States in 1789. He was hired by Moses Brown of Providence, R.I., to build a mill on the Pawtucket, or Seekonk, River. English laws forbade export of either the new machinery or plans for making it. Slater designed the machine from memory and built a mill that started operation in 1790. When the Napoleonic wars and the War of 1812 upset commerce and made English products difficult to obtain, more American investors began to build factories.

# PIONEER INDUSTRIES AND INVENTIONS

New England soon developed an important textile industry. It had swift streams for power and a humid climate, which kept cotton and wool fibers in condition for spinning and weaving. In Pennsylvania iron for machines, tools, and guns was smelted in stone furnaces. They burned charcoal, plentiful in this forested land. Spinning machines driven by steam were operating in New York by 1810. The first practical power loom was installed at Waltham, Mass., by Francis Cabot Lowell in 1814. Shoemaking was organized into a factory system of production in Massachusetts in the early 19th century. New England was the first area in the United States to industrialize.

American inventors produced many new machines that could be applied to industry as well as to agriculture. Oliver Evans designed a steam engine more powerful than that of James Watt. Engineers quickly adopted the new engine and used it to power locomotives and steamboats.

Cyrus McCormick invented several machines used to mechanize farming. His mechanical reaper, patented in 1834, revolutionized harvesting, making it quicker and easier. Elias Howe's sewing machine eased the life of the housewife and made the manufacture of clothing less expensive.

Techniques of factory production were refined in American workshops. Eli Whitney led the movement to standardize parts used in manufacture. They became interchangeable, enabling unskilled workers to assemble products from boxes of parts quickly. American factories used machine tools to make parts. These machines were arranged in lines for more efficient production. This was called the "American system of manufacturing," and it was admired by all other industrial nations. It was first applied to the manufacture of firearms and later spread to other industries like clock and lock making.

# ECONOMIC EFFECTS

Undergirding the development of modern Europe between the 1780s and 1849 was an unprecedented economic transformation that embraced the first stages of the great Industrial Revolution and a still more general expansion of commercial activity. Articulate Europeans were initially more impressed by the screaming political news generated by the French Revolution and ensuing Napoleonic Wars, but in retrospect the economic upheaval, which related in any event to political and diplomatic trends, has proved more fundamental.

Major economic change was spurred by western Europe's tremendous population growth during the late 18th century, extending well into the 19th century itself. Between 1750 and 1800, the populations of major countries increased between 50 and 100 percent, chiefly as a result of the use of new food crops (such as the potato) and a temporary decline in epidemic disease. Population growth of this magnitude compelled change. Peasant and artisanal children found their paths to inheritance blocked by sheer numbers and thus had to seek new forms of paying labour. Families of businessmen and landlords also had to innovate to take care of unexpectedly large surviving broods. These pressures occurred in a society already attuned to market transactions, possessed of an active merchant class, and blessed with considerable capital and access to overseas markets as a result of existing dominance in world trade.

Heightened commercialization showed in a number of areas. Vigorous peasants increased their landholdings, often at the expense of their less fortunate neighbours, who swelled the growing ranks of the near-propertyless. These peasants, in turn, produced food for sale in growing urban markets. Domestic manufacturing soared, as hundreds of thousands of rural producers worked full- or part-time to make thread and cloth, nails and tools under the sponsorship of urban merchants. Craft work in the cities began to shift toward production for distant markets, which encouraged artisan-owners to treat their journeymen less as fellow workers and more as wage labourers. Europe's social structure changed toward a basic division, both rural and urban, between owners and nonowners. Production expanded, leading by the end of the 18th century to a first wave of consumerism as rural wage earners began to purchase new kinds of commercially produced clothing, while urban middle-class families began to indulge in new tastes, such as uplifting books and educational toys for children.

In this context an outright industrial revolution took shape, led by Britain, which retained leadership in industrialization well past the middle of the 19th century. In 1840, British steam engines were generating 620,000 horsepower out of a European total of 860,000. Nevertheless, though delayed by the chaos of the French Revolution and Napoleonic Wars, many western

European nations soon followed suit; thus, by 1860 British steam-generated horsepower made up less than half the European total, with France, Germany, and Belgium gaining ground rapidly. Governments and private entrepreneurs worked hard to imitate British technologies after 1820, by which time an intense industrial revolution was taking shape in many parts of western Europe, particularly in coal-rich regions such as Belgium, northern France, and the Ruhr area of Germany. German pig iron production, a mere 40,000 tons in 1825, soared to 150,000 tons a decade later and reached 250,000 tons by the early 1850s. French coal and iron output doubled in the same span—huge changes in national capacities and the material bases of life.

Technological change soon spilled over from manufacturing into other areas. Increased production heightened demands on the transportation system to move raw materials and finished products. Massive road and canal building programs were one response, but steam engines also were directly applied as a result of inventions in Britain and the United States. Steam shipping plied major waterways soon after 1800 and by the 1840s spread to oceanic transport. Railroad systems, first developed to haul coal from mines, were developed for intercity transport during the 1820s; the first commercial line opened between Liverpool and Manchester in 1830. During the 1830s local rail networks fanned out in most western European countries, and national systems were planned in the following decade, to be completed by about 1870. In communication, the invention of the telegraph allowed faster exchange of news and commercial information than ever before.

New organization of business and labour was intimately linked to the new technologies. Workers in the industrialized sectors laboured in factories rather than in scattered shops or homes. Steam and water power required a concentration of labour close to the power source. Concentration of labour also allowed new discipline and specialization, which increased productivity.

The new machinery was expensive, and businessmen setting up even modest factories had to accumulate substantial capital through partnerships, loans from banks, or joint-stock ventures. While relatively small firms still predominated, and managerial bureaucracies were limited save in a few heavy industrial giants, a tendency toward expansion of the business unit was already noteworthy. Commerce was affected in similar ways, for new forms had to be devised to dispose of growing levels of production. Small shops replaced itinerant peddlers in villages and small towns. In Paris, the department store, introduced in the 1830s, ushered in an age of big business in the trading sector.

The speed of western Europe's Industrial Revolution should not be exaggerated. By 1850 in Britain, far and away the leader still, only half the total population lived in cities, and there were as many urban craft producers as there were factory hands. Relatively traditional economic sectors, in other words, did not disappear and even expanded in response to new needs for housing construction or food production. Nevertheless, the new economic sectors grew most rapidly, and even other branches displayed important new features as part of the general process of commercialization.

Geographic disparities complicate the picture as well. Belgium and, from the 1840s, many of the German states were well launched on an industrial revolution that brought them steadily closer to British levels. France, poorer in coal, concentrated somewhat more on increasing production in craft sectors, converting furniture making, for example, from an artistic endeavour to standardized output in advance of outright factory forms. Scandinavia and the Netherlands joined the industrial parade seriously only after 1850.

Southern and eastern Europe, while importing a few model factories and setting up some local rail lines, generally operated in a different economic orbit. City growth and technological change were both modest until much later in the 19th century, save in pockets of northern Italy and northern Spain. In eastern areas, western Europe's industrialization had its greatest impact in encouraging growing conversion to market agriculture, as Russia, Poland, and Hungary responded to grain import needs, particularly in the British Isles. As in eastern Prussia, the temptation was to impose new obligations on peasant serfs labouring on large estates, increasing the work requirements in order to meet export possibilities without fundamental technical change and without challenging the hold of the landlord class.

## SOCIAL UPHEAVAL

In western Europe, economic change produced massive social consequences during the first half of the 19th century. Basic aspects of daily life changed, and work was increasingly redefined. The intensity of change varied, of course—with factory workers affected most keenly, labourers on the land least—but some of the pressures were widespread.

For wage labourers, the autonomy of work declined; more people worked under the daily direction of others.

Early textile and metallurgical factories set shop rules, which urged workers to be on time, to stay at their machines rather than wandering around, and to avoid idle singing or chatter (difficult in any event given the noise of the equipment). These rules were increasingly enforced by foremen, who mediated between owners and ordinary labourers. Work speeded up. Machines set the pace, and workers were supposed to keep up: one French factory owner, who each week decorated the most productive machine (not its operators) with a garland of flowers, suggested where the priorities lay. Work, in other words, was to be fast, coordinated, and intense, without the admixture of distractions common in preindustrial labour. Some of these pressures spilled over to nonfactory settings as well, as craft directors tried to urge a higher productivity on journeymen artisans. Duration of work everywhere remained long, up to 14 hours a day, which was traditional but could be oppressive when work was more intense and walking time had to be added to reach the factories in the first place. Women and children were widely used for the less skilled operations; again, this was no novelty, but it was newly troubling now that work was located outside the home and was often more dangerous, given the hazards of unprotected machinery.

The nature of work shifted in the propertied classes as well. Middle-class people, not only factory owners but also merchants and professionals, began to trumpet a new work ethic. According to this ethic, work was the basic human good. He who worked was meritorious and should prosper, he who suffered did so because he did not work. Idleness and frivolity were officially frowned upon. Middle-class stories, for children and adults alike, were filled with uplifting tales of poor people who, by dint of assiduous work, managed to better themselves. In Britain, Samuel Smiles authored this kind of mobility literature, which was widely popular between the 1830s and 1860s. Between 1780 and 1840, Prussian school reading shifted increasingly toward praise of hard work as a means of social improvement, with corresponding scorn for laziness.

Shifts in work context had important implications for leisure. Businessmen who internalized the new work ethic felt literally uncomfortable when not on the job. Overall, the European middle class strove to redefine leisure tastes toward personal improvement and family cohesion; recreation that did not conduce to these ends was dubious. Family reading was a common pastime. Daughters were encouraged to learn piano playing, for music could draw the family together and demonstrate the refinement of its women. Through piano teaching, in turn, a new class of professional musicians began to emerge in the large cities. Middle-class people, newly wealthy, were willing to join in sponsorship of certain cultural events outside the home, such as symphony concerts. Book buying and newspaper reading also were supported, with a tendency to favour serious newspapers that focused on political and economic issues and books that had a certain classic status. Middle-class people also attended informative public lectures and night courses that might develop new work skills in such areas as applied science or management.

Middle-class pressures by no means totally reshaped popular urban leisure habits. Workers had limited time and means for play, but many absented themselves from the factories when they could afford to (often preferring free time over higher earnings, to the despair of their managers).

The sheer intensity of work constrained leisure nevertheless. Furthermore, city administrations tried to limit other traditional popular amusements, ranging from gambling to animal contests (bear-baiting, cockfighting) to popular festivals. Leisure of this sort was viewed as unproductive, crude, and—insofar as it massed urban crowds—dangerous to political order. Urban police forces, created during the 1820s in cities like London to provide more professional control over crime and public behaviour, spent much of their time combating popular leisure impulses during the middle decades of the 19th century. Popular habits did not fully accommodate to middle-class standards. Drinking, though disapproved of by middle-class critics, was an important recreational outlet, bringing men together in a semblance of community structure. Bars sprouted throughout working-class sections of town. On the whole, however, the early decades of the Industrial Revolution saw a massive decline of popular leisure traditions; even in the countryside, festivals were diluted by importing paid entertainers from the cities. Leisure did not disappear, but it was increasingly reshaped toward respectable family pastimes or spectatorship at inexpensive concerts or circuses, where large numbers of people paid professional entertainers to take their minds away from the everyday routine.

The growth of cities and industry had a vital impact on family life. The family declined as a production unit as work moved away from home settings. This was true not only for workers but also for middle-class people. Many businessmen setting up a new store or factory in the 1820s initially assumed that their wives would assist them, in the time-honoured fashion in which all family members were expected to pitch in. After the first generation, however, this impulse faded, in part because fashionable homes were located at some distance from commercial sections and needed separate attention. In general, most urban groups tended to respond to the separation of home and work by redefining gender roles, so that married men became the family breadwinners (aided, in the working class, by older children) and women were the domestic specialists.

In the typical working-class family, women were expected to work from their early teens through marriage a decade or so later. The majority of women workers in the cities went into domestic service in middle-class households, but an important minority laboured in factories; another minority became prostitutes. Some women continued working outside the home after marriage, but most pulled back to tasks, such as laundering, that could be done domestically. Their other activities concentrated on shopping for the family (an arduous task on limited budgets), caring for children, and maintaining contacts with other relatives who might support the family socially and provide aid during economic hardships.

Few middle-class women worked in paid employment at any point in their lives. Managing a middle-class household was complex, even with a servant present. Standards of child rearing urged increased maternal attention, and women were also supposed to provide a graceful and comfortable tone for family life. Middle-class ideals held the family to be a sacred place and women its chief agents because of their innate morality and domestic devotion. Men owed the family good manners and the provision of economic security, but their daily interactions became increasingly peripheral. Many middle-class families also began, in the early 19th century, to limit their birth rate, mainly through increasing sexual abstinence. Having too many children could complicate the family's economic well-being and prevent the necessary attention and support for the children who were desired. The middle class thus pioneered a new definition of family size that would ultimately become more widespread in European society.

New family arrangements, both for workers and for middle-class people, suggested new courtship patterns. As wage earners having no access to property, urban workers were increasingly able to form liaisons early in life without waiting for inheritance and without close supervision by a watchful community. Sexual activity began earlier in life than had been standard before the 1780s. Marriage did not necessarily follow, for many workers moved from job to job and some unquestionably exploited female partners who were eager for more durable arrangements. Rates of illegitimate births began to rise rapidly throughout western Europe from about 1780 (from 2 to 4 up to 10 percent of total births) among young rural as well as urban workers. Sexual pleasure, or its quest, became more important for young adults. Similar symptoms developed among some middle-class men, who exploited female servants or the growing numbers of brothels that dotted the large cities and that often did exceptional business during school holidays. Respectable young middle-class women held back from these trends. They were, however, increasingly drawn to beliefs in a romantic marriage, which became part of the new family ideal. Marriage age for middle-class women also dropped, creating an age disparity between men and women in the families of this class. Economic criteria for family formation remained important in many social sectors, but young people enjoyed more freedom in courtship, and other factors, sexual or emotional or both, gained increasing legitimacy.

Changes in family life, rooted in shifts in modes of livelihood and methods of work, had substantial impact on all family members. Older people gained new roles, particularly in working-class families, where they helped out as baby-sitters for grandchildren. Women's economic power in the family decreased. Many groups of men argued vigorously that women should stick to family concerns. By the 1830s and '40s one result was the inception of laws that regulated women's hours of work (while leaving men free from protection or constraints); this was a humanitarian move to protect women's family roles, but it also reduced women's economic opportunities on grounds of their special frailty. The position of children also began to be redefined. Middle-class ideals held that children were innocents, to be educated and nurtured. Most working-class families urged a more traditional view of children as contributors to the family economy, but they too could see advantages in sending their children to school where possible and restricting their work in dangerous factories. Again, after the first decades of industrialization, reform laws began to respond. Legislation in Britain, France, and Prussia during the 1830s restricted the employment of young children in the factories and encouraged school attendance.

Along with its impact on daily patterns of life and family institutions, economic change began to shift Europe's social structure and create new antagonisms among urban social classes. The key division lay between the members

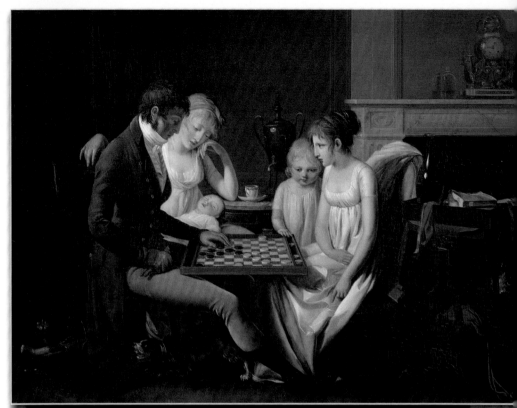

*THE FAMILY CHANGED BECAUSE OF THE INDUSTRIAL REVOLUTION. MIDDLE-CLASS FAMILIES ALLOWED CHILDREN TO STUDY AND PLAY.*

of the middle class, who owned businesses or acquired professional education, and those of the working class, who depended on the sale of labour for a wage. Neither group was homogeneous. Many middle-class people criticized the profit-seeking behaviour of the new factory owners. Artisans often shunned factory workers and drew distinctions based on their traditional prestige and (usually) greater literacy. Some skilled workers, earning good wages, emulated middle-class people, seeking education and acquiring domestic trappings such as pianos.

Nevertheless, the social divide was considerable. It increasingly affected residential patterns, as wealthier classes moved away from the crowded slums of the poor, in contrast to the greater mixture in the quarters of preindustrial cities. Middle-class people deplored the work and sexual habits of many workers, arguing that their bad behaviour was the root cause of poverty. City governments enacted harsh measures against beggars, while new national laws attempted to make charity harder to obtain. The British Poor Law Reform of 1834, in particular, tightened the limits on relief in hopes of forcing able-bodied workers to fend for themselves.

Class divisions manifested themselves in protest movements. Middle-class people joined political protests hoping to win new rights against aristocratic monopoly. Workers increasingly organized on their own despite the fact that new laws banned craft organizations and outlawed unions and strikes. Some workers attacked the reliance on machinery in the name of older, more humane traditions of work. Luddite protests of this sort began in Britain during the decade 1810–20. More numerous were groups of craft workers, and some factory hands, who formed incipient trade unions to demand better conditions as well as to provide mutual aid in cases of sickness or other setbacks. National union movements arose in Britain during the 1820s, though they ultimately failed. Huge strikes in the silk industry around Lyon, France, in 1831 and 1834 sought a living minimum wage for all workers. The most ambitious worker movements tended to emphasize a desire to turn back the clock to older work systems where there was

*LUDDITES TOOK OUT THEIR FRUSTRATIONS ABOUT THE CHANGING TIMES ON THE MACHINES THEY FEARED WOULD SOON REPLACE THEM.*

greater equality and a greater commitment to craft skill, but most failed. Smaller, local unions did achieve some success in preserving the conditions of the traditional systems. Social protest was largely intermittent because many workers were too poor or too disoriented to mount a larger effort, but it clearly signaled important tensions in the new economic order.

Connections between political change and socioeconomic upheaval were real but complex. Economic grievances associated with early industrialization fed into later revolutions, particularly the outbursts in 1848, but the newest social classes were not prime bearers of the revolutionary message. Revolutions also resulted from new political ideas directed against the institutions and social arrangements of the preindustrial order. Their results facilitated further economic change, but this was not necessarily their intent. Political unrest must be seen as a discrete factor shaping a new Europe along with fundamental economic forces.

# THE SECOND INDUSTRIAL REVOLUTION AND A CHANGING SOCIETY

A s during the previous half century, much of the framework for Europe's history following 1850 was set by rapidly changing social and economic patterns, which extended to virtually the entire continent. In western Europe, shifts were less dramatic than they had been at the onset of the Industrial Revolution, but they posed important challenges to older traditions and to early industrial behaviours alike. In Russia, initial industrialization contributed to literally revolutionary tensions soon after 1900.

The geographic spread of the Industrial Revolution was important in its own right. Germany's industrial output began to surpass that of Britain by the 1870s, especially in heavy industry. The United States became a major industrial power, competing actively with Europe; American agriculture also began to compete as steamships, canning, and refrigeration altered the terms of international trade in foodstuffs. Russia and Japan, though less vibrant competitors by 1900, entered the lists, while significant industrialization began in parts of Italy, Austria, and Scandinavia. These developments were compatible with increased economic growth in older industrial centres, but they did produce an atmosphere of rivalry and uncertainty even in prosperous years.

# ANOTHER INDUSTRIAL REVOLUTION

The machines of the Industrial Revolution in the 18th and early 19th centuries were simple, mechanical devices compared with the industrial technology that followed. Many new products were devised, and important advances were made in the system of mass production. Changes in industry were so great that the period after 1860 has been called the Second Industrial Revolution. New scientific knowledge was applied to industry as scientists and engineers unlocked the secrets of physics and chemistry. Great new industries were founded on this scientific advance: steel, chemicals, and petroleum benefited from new understandings of chemistry; breakthroughs in the study of electricity and magnetism provided the basis for a large electrical industry. These new industries were larger and more productive than any industries existing before. Germany and the United States became the leaders, and by the end of the 19th century they were challenging Great Britain in the world market for industrial goods.

Throughout the most advanced industrial zone (from Britain through Germany) the second half of the 19th century was also marked by a new round of technological change. New processes of iron smelting such as that involving the use of the Bessemer converter (invented in 1856) expanded steel production by allowing more automatic introduction of alloys and in general increased the scale of heavy industrial operations. The development of electrical and internal combustion engines allowed transmission of power even outside factory centres. The result was a rise of sweatshop industries that used sewing machines for clothing manufacturing; the spread of powered equipment to artisanal production, on construction sites, in bakeries and other food-processing centres (some of which saw the advent of factories); and the use of powered equipment on the larger agricultural estates and for processes such as cream separation in the dairy industry. In factories themselves, a new round of innovation by the 1890s brought larger looms to the textile industry and automatic processes to shoe manufacture and machine- and shipbuilding (through automatic riveters) that reduced skill requirements and greatly increased per capita production. Technological transformation was virtually universal in industrial societies. Work speeded up still further, semi-skilled operatives became increasingly characteristic,

*STEEL PRODUCTION INCREASED CONSIDERABLY DUE TO THE INVENTION OF THE BESSEMER CONVERTER.*

and, on the plus side, production and thus prosperity reached new heights.

Organizational changes matched the "second industrial revolution" in technology. More expensive equipment, plus economies made possible by increasing scale, promoted the formation of larger businesses. All western European countries eased limits on the formation of joint-stock corporations from

**89**

the 1850s, and the rate of corporate growth was breathtaking by the end of the century. Giant corporations grouped together to influence the terms of trade, especially in countries such as Germany, where cartels controlled as much as 90 percent of production in the electrical equipment and chemical industries. Big business techniques had a direct impact on labour. Increasingly, engineers set production quotas, displacing not only individual workers but also foremen by introducing time-and-motion procedures designed to maximize efficiency.

# THE IMPACT OF DEVELOPING INDUSTRIES

The age of electricity began in 1882 when Thomas A. Edison introduced a system of electric lighting in New York City. Electricity was later applied to driving all kinds of machinery as well as powering locomotives and streetcars. Electric lighting quickly spread across the United States and was soon adopted in Europe. The electrical industry was dominated by large companies that developed new products and then manufactured and marketed them. These companies were based in Germany and the United States but sold their goods all over the world. They were the first multinational companies. Companies like Westinghouse and General Electric helped to electrify cities in Europe, Africa, and South America.

The steel and chemical industries used new technology that greatly increased production. The size of factories increased rapidly, employing more workers and using

# THOMAS EDISON

Thomas Alva Edison was the quintessential American inventor in the era of Yankee ingenuity. Born in 1847 in Ohio, he began his career in 1863, during the adolescence of the telegraph industry, when virtually the only source of electricity was primitive batteries putting out a low-voltage current. Before he died, in 1931, he had played a critical role in introducing the modern age of electricity. From his labouratories and workshops emanated the phonograph, the carbon-button transmitter for the telephone speaker and microphone, the incandescent lamp, a revolutionary generator of unprecedented efficiency, the first commercial electric light and power system, an experimental electric railroad, and key elements of motion-picture apparatus, as well as a host of other inventions.

Edison was the seventh and last child—the fourth surviving—of Samuel Edison, Jr., and Nancy Elliot Edison. At an early age he developed hearing problems, which have been variously attributed but were most likely due to a familial tendency to mastoiditis. Whatever the cause, Edison's deafness strongly influenced his behaviour and career, providing the motivation for many of his inventions.

After inventing the phonograph, Edison next focused his efforts on producing an electric light to replace gas lighting. Although electric lighting had existed since the early 19th century, it was not yet practical for home use. Edison's aim was to invent a lamp that would become incandescent, or luminous, as a result of heat passing through it.

Edison made filaments, or threads, of many heat-resistant materials into glass globes. The heat crumbled the filaments into ashes. Later he pumped air out of the bulbs. Using platinum filaments in these vacuum bulbs, he had some success. But he needed an inexpensive substance to use for filaments. He continued his research for many months.

(*continued on the next page*)

## THOMAS EDISON (CONTINUED)

In October 1879 Edison introduced the modern age of light. In his labouratory he tensely watched a charred cotton thread glow for 40 hours in a vacuum bulb. He knew then that he had invented the first commercially practical incandescent electric light. In his continuing search for a filament that would work better than the cotton thread, carbonized bamboo seemed most successful. For nine years millions of Edison lamp bulbs were

*THOMAS EDISON WORKED ON DEVELOPING THE INCANDESCENT LIGHT BULB FROM HIS NEW JERSEY LABORATORY.*

made with bamboo filaments. In time, however, the modern filament of drawn tungsten wire was developed.

Edison also devoted his energies to improving the dynamo to furnish the necessary power for electric lighting systems. In addition, he developed a complete system of distributing the current and built the first central power station in lower Manhattan in 1882.

To work on the power system, Edison moved his operations from Menlo Park to New York City, where his wife died in 1884. A widower with three young children, Edison married Mina Miller in 1886. They also had three children. Edison died in West Orange, New Jersey, on Oct. 18, 1931. His West Orange labouratory and his 23-room home, Glenmont, were designated a national historic site in 1955. The labouratory is exactly as he left it. It includes his library, papers, and early models of many of his inventions.

more machinery. These industries integrated all stages of production under a single corporate structure. They bought out competitors and acquired sources of raw materials and retail outlets. Corporations such as U.S. Steel and Standard Oil controlled all stages of manufacturing the product, from mining and drilling to delivering it to the customer. This gave them great economic power, and the United States government took measures to limit their monopolies in steel and petroleum.

The larger size of business presented great challenges to managers who administered enormous organizations with many branches and subsidiaries. Advances in communications and transportation helped decision makers to maintain control. The electric telegraph was invented by Samuel Morse in 1844 and was used to relay commercial information about prices and markets. It was used in the stock exchanges and on the railway systems. Alexander Graham Bell patented his telephone in 1876, and networks of telephone lines were built quickly across the United States.

The telephone became a useful tool for managers to keep in contact with the widely dispersed parts of their businesses. New methods of management were devised that stressed central control, planning, and efficient production methods. One of the leading advocates of "scientific management" was Frederick Winslow Taylor.

# MASS PRODUCTION

The Second Industrial Revolution marked great progress in the methods of mass production. More and more industries used interchangeable parts and machine tools. Electric power replaced steam power in factories; it was cheaper, faster, and more flexible. It allowed machine tools to be arranged more efficiently. Human power was replaced by machine power.

In 1881, at the Midvale Steel Company in the United States, Frederick W. Taylor began studies of the organization of manufacturing operations that subsequently formed the foundation of modern production planning. After carefully studying the smallest parts of simple tasks, such as the shoveling of dry materials, Taylor was able to design methods and tools that permitted workers to produce significantly more with less physical effort. Later, by making detailed stopwatch measurements of the time required to perform each step of manufacture, Taylor brought a quantitative approach to the organization of production functions.

# FREDERICK WINSLOW TAYLOR

Frederick W. Taylor (1856–1915) was forced to abandon plans for matriculation to Harvard, as his eyesight had deteriorated from night study. With sight restored in 1875, he was apprenticed to learn the trades of patternmaker and machinist at the Enterprise Hydraulic Works in Philadelphia.

Three years later he went to the Midvale Steel Company, where, starting as a machine shop labourer, he became successively shop clerk, machinist, gang boss, foreman, maintenance foreman, head of the drawing office, and chief engineer.

In 1881, at 25, he introduced time study at the Midvale plant. The profession of time study was founded on the success of this project, which also formed the basis of Taylor's subsequent theories of management science. Essentially, Taylor suggested that production efficiency in a shop or factory could be greatly enhanced by close observation of the individual worker and elimination of waste time and motion in his operation. Though the Taylor system provoked resentment and opposition from labour when carried to extremes, its value in rationalizing production was indisputable and its impact on the development of mass-production techniques immense.

Studying at night, Taylor earned a degree in mechanical engineering from Stevens Institute of Technology in 1883. The following year he became chief engineer at Midvale and completed the design and construction of a novel machine shop. Taylor might have enjoyed a brilliant full-time career as an inventor—he had more than 40 patents to his credit—but his interest in what was soon called scientific management led him to resign his post at Midvale and to become general manager of the Manufacturing Investment Company (1890–93), which in turn led him to develop a "new profession, that of consulting engineer in management." He served a long list of prominent

(*continued on the next page*)

# FREDERICK WINSLOW TAYLOR
## (CONTINUED)

firms ending with the Bethlehem Steel Corporation; while at Bethlehem, he developed high-speed steel and performed notable experiments in shoveling and pig-iron handling.

Taylor retired at age 45 but continued to devote time and money to promote the principles of scientific management through lectures at universities and professional societies. From 1904 to 1914, with his wife and three adopted children, Taylor lived in Philadelphia. The American Society of Mechanical Engineers elected him president in 1906, the same year that he was awarded an honorary doctor of science degree by the University of Pennsylvania. Many of his influential publications first appeared in the *Transactions* of that society. *The Principles of Scientific Management* was published commercially in 1911.

Taylor's fame increased after his testimony in 1912 at the hearings before a special committee of the House of Representatives to investigate his own and other systems of shop management. Considering himself a reformer, he continued expounding the ideals and principles of his system of management until his death.

At the same time, Frank B. Gilbreth and his wife, Lillian M. Gilbreth, U.S. industrial engineers, began their pioneering studies of the movements by which people carry out tasks. Using the then new technology of motion pictures, the Gilbreths analyzed the design of motion patterns and work areas with a view to achieving maximum economy of effort. The "time-and-motion" studies of Taylor and the Gilbreths provided important tools for the design of contemporary manufacturing systems.

In 1916 Henri Fayol, who for many years had managed a large coal mining company in France, began publishing his ideas about the organization and supervision of work, and by 1925 he had enunciated several principles and functions of management. His idea of unity of command, which stated that an employee should receive orders from only one supervisor, helped to clarify the organizational structure of many manufacturing operations.

Much of the credit for bringing these early concepts together in a coherent form, and creating the modern, integrated, mass production operation, belongs to the U.S. industrialist Henry Ford and his colleagues at the Ford Motor Company, where in 1913 a moving-belt conveyor was used in the assembly of flywheel magnetos. With it assembly time was cut from 18 minutes per magneto to 5 minutes. The approach was then applied to automobile body and motor assembly. Parts were assembled on a moving conveyor belt, and the Model T took shape as it moved from one work station to the next. The design of these production lines was highly analytical and sought the optimum division of tasks among work stations, optimum line speed, optimum work height, and careful synchronization of simultaneous operations.

The success of Ford's operation led to the adoption of mass production principles by industry in the United States and Europe. The methods made major contributions to the large growth in manufacturing productivity that has characterized the 20th century and produced phenomenal increases in material wealth and improvements in living standards in the industrialized countries.

The efficiencies of mass production result from a careful, systematic application of ideas and concepts. The following summary lists the basic principles of mass production:

1. The careful division of the total production operation into specialized tasks comprising relatively simple, highly repetitive motion patterns and minimal handling or positioning of the workpiece. This permits the development of human motion patterns that are easily learned and rapidly performed with a minimum of unnecessary motion or mental readjustment.

2. The simplification and standardization of component parts to permit large production runs of parts that are readily fitted to other parts without adjustment. The imposition of other standards (e.g., dimensional tolerances, parts location, material types, stock thickness, common fasteners, packaging material) on all parts of the product further increases the economies that can be achieved.

3. The development and use of specialized machines, materials, and processes. The selection of materials and development of tools and machines for each operation minimizes the amount of human effort required, maximizes the output per unit of capital investment, reduces the number of off-standard units produced, and reduces raw material costs.

4. The systematic engineering and planning of the total production process permit the best balance between human effort and machinery, the most effective division of labour and specialization of skills, and the total integration of the production system to optimize productivity and minimize costs.

Careful, skilled industrial engineering and management are required to achieve the maximum benefits that application of

# HENRY FORD

In 1896 a horseless carriage chugged along the streets of Detroit, with crowds gathering whenever it appeared. Terrified horses ran at its approach. The police tried to curb this nuisance by forcing its driver, Henry Ford, to get a license. That car was the first of many millions produced by the automotive pioneer.

Henry Ford was born near Dearborn, Mich., on July 30, 1863. His mother died when he was 12. He helped on the family farm in summer and in winter attended a one-room school. Watches and clocks fascinated the boy. He went around the countryside doing repair work without pay, merely for the chance to tinker with machinery.

At 16 Ford walked to Detroit and apprenticed himself to a mechanic for $2.50 a week. His board was $3.50, so he worked four hours every night for a watchmaker for $2 a week. Later he worked in an engine shop and set up steam engines used on farms. In 1884 he took charge of a farm his father gave him. He married and seemed settled down, but after two years he went back to Detroit and worked as night engineer for the Detroit Edison Company.

Ford built his first car in a little shed behind his home. It had a two-cylinder engine over the rear axle that developed four horsepower, a single seat fitted in a boxlike body, an electric bell for a horn, and a steering lever instead of a wheel. In 1899 Ford helped organize the Detroit Automobile Company, which built cars to order. Ford wanted to build in quantity at a price within the reach of many. His partners objected, and Ford withdrew.

In 1903 he organized the Ford Motor Company with only $28,000 raised in cash. This money came from 11 other stockholders. One investor put just $2,500 into Ford's venture (only $1,000 of it in cash). He drew more than $5,000,000 in dividends, and he received more than $30,000,000 when he sold all of his holdings to Ford in 1919.

(*continued on the next page*)

# HENRY FORD (CONTINUED)

Early automobile manufacturers merely bought automobile parts and assembled the cars. Ford's objective was to make every part that went into his cars. He acquired iron and coal mines, forests, mills, and factories to produce and shape his steel and alloys, his fuel, wood, glass, and leather. He built railroad and steamship lines and an airplane freight service in order to transport his products.

Mass production was Ford's main idea, and he replaced men with machines wherever possible. Each man was given only one task, which he did repeatedly until it became automatic. Conveyors brought the job to the man instead of having the man waste time going to the job. To cut shipping costs, parts were shipped from the main plants in the Detroit area and assembled into cars at branch plants.

Ford also won fame as a philanthropist and pacifist. He established an eight-hour workday, a minimum wage of $5 daily (later raised to $6), and a five-day week. He built a hospital in Detroit with fixed rates for service and physicians and nurses on salary. He created the Edison Institute, which includes Greenfield Village and the Edison Institute Museum and trade schools. Independence Hall, Thomas Edison's early labouratory, and other famous old buildings were reproduced in the village, which is open to the public. During World War I Ford headed a party of pacifists to Norway in a failed attempt to end the war, but during both World War I and World War II his company was a major producer of war materials.

In 1945 Ford yielded the presidency of the company to his 28-year-old grandson, Henry Ford II. Ford died on April 7, 1947, at the age of 83. Most of his personal estate, valued at about $205,000,000, was left to the Ford Foundation, one of the world's largest public trusts.

these principles can provide. Planning begins with the original design of the product; raw materials and component parts must be adaptable to production and handling by mass techniques. The entire production process is planned in detail, including the flows of materials and information throughout the process.

*FORD MOTOR COMPANY PLANT, RIVER ROUGE, WEST OF DETROIT, MICHIGAN, C. 1930S. BUILT BETWEEN 1917 AND 1925, IT BECAME THE MODEL FOR ASSEMBLY-LINE PRODUCTION, TURNING PARTS AT ONE END INTO FINISHED CARS AT THE OTHER.*

Production volume must be carefully estimated because the selection of techniques depends upon the volume to be produced and anticipated short-term changes in demand. Volume must be large enough, first, to permit the task to be divided into its sub-elements and assigned to different individuals; second, to justify the substantial capital investment often required for specialized machines and processes; and third, to permit large production runs so that human effort and capital are efficiently employed.

The need for detailed advance planning extends beyond the production system itself. The large, continuous flow of product from the factory requires equally well-planned distribution and marketing operations to bring the product to the consumer. Advertising, market research, transportation problems, licensing, and tariffs must all be considered in establishing a mass production operation. Thus, mass production planning implies a complete system plan from raw material to consumer.

In addition to lowering cost, the application of the principles of mass production led to major improvements in uniformity and quality. The large volume, standardized design, and standardized materials and processes facilitate statistical control and inspection techniques to monitor production and control quality. This leads to assurance that quality levels are achieved without incurring the large costs that would be necessary for detailed inspection of all products.

# MODIFICATIONS IN SOCIAL STRUCTURE

Developments in technology and organization reshaped social structure. A recognizable peasantry continued to exist in western

Europe, but it increasingly had to adapt to new methods. In many areas (most notably, the Netherlands and Denmark) a cooperative movement spread to allow peasants to market dairy goods and other specialties to the growing urban areas without abandoning individual landownership. Many peasants began to achieve new levels of education and to adopt innovations such as new crops, better seeds, and fertilizers; they also began to innovate politically, learning to press governments to protect their agricultural interests.

In the cities the working classes continued to expand, and distinctions between artisans and factory workers, though real, began to fade. A new urban class emerged as sales outlets proliferated and growing managerial bureaucracies (both private and public) created the need for secretaries, bank tellers, and other clerical workers. A lower middle class, composed of salaried personnel who could boast a certain level of education— indeed, whose jobs depended on literacy—and who worked in conditions different from manufacturing labourers, added an important ingredient to European society and politics. Though their material conditions differed little from those of some factory workers, though they too were subject to bosses and to challenging new technologies such as typewriters and cash registers, most white-collar workers shunned association with blue-collar ranks. Big business employers encouraged this separation by setting up separate payment systems and benefit programs, for they were eager to avoid a union of interests that might augment labour unrest.

At the top of European society a new upper class formed as big business took shape, representing a partial amalgam of aristocratic landowners and corporate magnates. This upper class wielded immense political influence, for example, in supporting government armaments buildups that provided markets for heavy industrial goods and jobs for aristocratic military officers.

Along with modifications in social structure came important shifts in popular behaviour, some of them cutting across class lines. As a result of growing production, prosperity increased throughout most of western Europe. Major economic recessions interrupted this prosperity, as factory output could outstrip demand and as investment speculation could, relatedly, outstrip real economic gains. Speculative bank crises and economic downturns occurred in the mid-1850s and particularly in the middle years of both the 1870s and '90s, causing substantial hardship and even wider uncertainty. Nevertheless, the general trend in standards of living for most groups was upward, allowing ordinary people to improve their diets and housing and maintain a small margin for additional purchases. The success of mass newspapers, for example, which reached several million subscribers by the 1890s, depended on the ability to pay as well as on literacy. A bicycle craze, beginning among the middle classes in the 1880s and gradually spreading downward, represented a consumer passion for a more expensive item. Improvement in standards of living was aided by a general reduction in the birth rate, which developed rapidly among urban workers and even peasants. Families increasingly regarded children as an expense, to be weighed against other possibilities, and altered traditional behaviour accordingly. Reduction in the birth rate was achieved in part by sexual abstinence but also by the use of birth control devices, which had been widely available since the vulcanization of rubber in the 1840s, and by illegal abortions, while infanticide continued in rural areas. Completing the installation of a new demographic regime was a rapid decline in infant mortality after 1880.

Rising living standards were accompanied by increased leisure time. Workers pressed for a workday of 12, then 10 hours, and shortly after 1900 a few groups began to demand an even shorter period. Scattered vacation days also were introduced, and the "English weekend," which allowed time off on Saturday afternoons as well as Sundays, spread widely. Middle-class groups, for their part, loosened their previous work ethic in order to accommodate a wider range of leisure activities.

The second half of the 19th century witnessed the birth of modern leisure in western Europe and, to an extent, beyond. Team sports were played in middle-class schools and through a variety of amateur and professional teams. Many sports, such as soccer (football), had originated in traditional games but now gained standardized rules, increasing specialization among players, and the impassioned record-keeping appropriate to an industrial age. Sports commanded widespread participation among various social groups and served as the basis for extensive commercial operations. Huge stadiums and professional leagues signaled the advent of a new level of spectatorship. While many sports primarily focused on male interests, women began to participate in tennis and entire families in pastimes such as croquet and bicycling.

Leisure options were by no means confined to sports. Mass newspapers emphasized entertaining feature stories rather than politics. Parks and museums open to the public became standard urban features. Train excursions to beaches won wide patronage from factory workers as well as middle-class vacationers. A popular theatre expanded in the cities; British music-hall, typical of the genre, combined song and satire, poking fun at life's tribulations and providing an escapist emphasis on pleasure-seeking. After 1900, similar themes spilled into the new visual technology that soon coalesced into early motion pictures.

# THE RISE OF ORGANIZED
# LABOUR AND MASS PROTESTS

Mass leisure coexisted interestingly with the final major social development of the later 19th century, the escalating forms of class conflict. Pressed by the rapid pace and often dulling routine of work, antagonized by a faceless corporate management structure seemingly bent on efficiency at all costs, workers in various categories developed more active protest modes in the later 19th century. They were aided by their growing familiarity with basic industrial conditions, which facilitated the formation of relevant demands and made organization more feasible. Legal changes, spreading widely in western Europe after 1870, reduced political barriers to unionization and strikes, though clashes with government forces remained a common part of labour unrest.

Not surprisingly, given the mood of reaction following the failures of the 1848 revolutions, the 1850s constituted a period of relative placidity in labour relations. Skilled workers in Britain formed a conservative craft union movement, known as New Model Unionism, that urged calm negotiation and respectability; a number of durable trade unions were formed as a result, and a minority of workers gained experience in national organization. Miners and factory workers rose in strikes occasionally, signaling a class-based tension with management in many areas, but no consistent pattern developed.

The depression of the 1870s, which brought new hardship and reminded workers of the uncertainty of their lot, encouraged a wider range of agitation, and by the 1890s mass unionism surfaced throughout western Europe. Not only artisans but also factory workers and relatively unskilled groups, such as dockers, showed a growing ability to form national unions that made use of the sheer power of numbers, even in default of special skills, to press for gains. Strike rates increased steadily. In 1892 French workers struck 261 times against 500 companies; most of the efforts remained small and local, and only 50,000 workers were involved. By 1906, the peak French strike year before 1914, 1,309 strikes brought 438,000 workers off the job. British and German strike rates were higher still; in Britain, more than 2,000,000 workers struck between 1909 and 1913. A number of nationwide strikes showed labour's new muscle.

Unionization formed the second prong of the new labour surge. Along with mass unions in individual industries, general federations formed at the national level, such as the British Trades Union Congress and the French and Italian general confederations of labour. Unions provided social and material benefits for members along with their protest action; in many industries they managed to win collective bargaining procedures with employers, though this was far from a uniform pattern in an atmosphere of bitter competition over management rights; and they could influence governmental decisions in the labour area.

The rise of organized labour signaled an unprecedented development in the history of European popular protest. Never before had so many people been formally organized; never before had withdrawal of labour served as the chief protest weapon. Many workers joined a sweeping ideological fervor to their protest. Many were socialists, and a number of trade union movements were tightly linked to the rising socialist parties; this was particularly true in Germany and Austria. In other areas, especially France and Italy, an alternative syndicalist ideology won many adherents in the union movement; syndicalists urged that direct action through strikes should topple governments

*THROUGH LABOUR UNIONS AND STRIKES, WORKERS COULD ATTAIN BETTER WORKING CONDITIONS.*

and usher in a new age in which organizations of workers would control production. Against these varied revolutionary currents, many workers saw in unions and strikes primarily a means to compensate for changes in their work environment, through higher pay (as a reward for less pleasant labour) and shorter hours. Even here, there was an ability to seek new ends rather than appealing to past standards. Overall, pragmatism battled with ideology in most labour movements, and in point of fact none of the large organizations aimed primarily at revolution.

Labour unrest was not the only form of protest in the later 19th century. In many continental nations (but not in Britain or Scandinavia), nationalist organizations drew the attention of discontented shopkeepers and others in the lower middle class who felt pressed by new business forms, such as department stores and elabourate managerial bureaucracies, but who were also hostile to socialism and the union movement. Nationalist riots surfaced periodically in many countries around such issues as setbacks in imperialist competition or internal political scandals. Some of the riots and accompanying organizations were also anti-Semitic, holding Jews responsible for big business and socialism alike. France witnessed the most important agitation from the radical right, through organizations like the Action Française; but anti-Semitic political movements also developed in Germany and Austria.

Important women's movements completed the new roster of mass protests. The basic conditions of women did not change greatly in western Europe during the second half of the 19th century, with the significant exception of the rapidly declining birth rate. The steady spread of primary education increased female literacy, bringing it nearly equal to male levels by 1900. A growing minority of middle-class women also entered secondary schools, and by the 1870s a handful reached universities and professional schools. Several separate women's colleges were founded in centres such as Oxford and Cambridge, and, against heavy resistance, a few women became doctors and lawyers. For somewhat larger numbers of women, new jobs in the service sector of the economy, such as telephone operators, primary-school teachers, and nurses, provided opportunities for work before marriage. Gradually some older sectors of employment, such as domestic service, began to decline. Nevertheless,

*SOME WOMEN FOUGHT FOR THE RIGHT TO EDUCATION, EMPLOYMENT, AND THE VOTE.*

emphasis on a domestic sphere for women changed little. Public schools, while teaching literacy, also taught the importance of household skills and support for a working husband.

These were the circumstances that produced increasingly active feminist movements, sometimes independently and sometimes in association with socialist parties. Feminist leaders sought greater equality under the law, an attack on a double-standard sexuality that advantaged men. Above all, they came to concentrate on winning the vote. Massive petitions in Britain, accompanied by considerable violence after 1900, signaled Europe's most active feminist movement, drawing mainly on middle-class ranks. Feminists in Scandinavia were successful in winning voting rights after 1900. Almost everywhere, feminist pressures added to the new variety of mass protest action.

# INDUSTRIALIZATION TO POSTINDUSTRIALIZATION

By the outbreak of World War I in 1914, only a small number of industries in the most developed nations of the world had adopted advanced production methods and organization. Much of the world had not yet begun a first industrial revolution. Russia, Canada, Italy, and Japan were just beginning to industrialize. Only Great Britain, the United States, Germany, France, and some parts of the Scandinavian countries had successfully completed an industrial revolution. China, India, and Spain did not begin to industrialize until well into the 20th century.

The 19th century had itself seen the culmination of the Industrial Revolution that had begun in the 18th century, but the transformation wrought by steam power, steel, machine-made textiles, and rail communications was only the beginning. Still more rapid and spectacular changes came with further advances in science and technology: electricity, telegraphy and telephony, radio and television, subatomic physics, oil and petrochemicals, plastics, jet engines, computers, telematics, and bioengineering.

The development of technology, in particular, would not have been possible without a more skilled and better educated work force. In most European countries during this period, education was extended both to more of the population and to a later age, and the numbers entering higher education greatly increased. Women began to gain access to more of the opportunities hitherto monopolized by men.

If this was a process of social leveling upward, the same process began to affect the social classes themselves. While European society remained more hierarchical than that in the United States, there began to be both greater social mobility and fewer blatant class differences as expressed in clothes, behaviour, and speech. A "mass society" began to share mass pleasures. Apparent homogeneity, both vertically within societies and horizontally between them, was accelerated by the cinema, radio, and television, each offering attractive role models to be imitated or, by older generations, deplored. Some referred to this process as "the Americanization of Europe."

Following the Industrial Revolution came a postindustrial society. This is a society marked by a transition from a manufacturing-based economy to a service-based economy, a transition that is also connected with subsequent societal restructuring. Postindustrialization is the next evolutionary step from an industrialized society and is most evident in countries and regions that were among the first to experience the Industrial Revolution, such as the United States, western Europe, and Japan.

American sociologist Daniel Bell first coined the term "postindustrial" in 1973 in his book *The Coming of Post-Industrial Society: A Venture in Social Forecasting,* which describes several features of a postindustrial society. Postindustrial societies are characterized by:

1. A transition from the production of goods to the production of services, with very few firms directly manufacturing any goods.

2. The replacement of blue-collar manual labourers with technical and professional workers—such as computer engineers, doctors, and bankers—as the direct production of goods is moved elsewhere.

3. The replacement of practical knowledge with theoretical knowledge.

4. Greater attention being paid to the theoretical and ethical implications of new technologies, which helps society avoid some of the negative features of introducing new technologies, such as environmental accidents and massive widespread power outages.

5. The development of newer scientific disciplines—such as those that involve new forms of information technology, cybernetics, or artificial intelligence—to assess the theoretical and ethical implications of new technologies.

6. A stronger emphasis on the university and polytechnic institutes, which produce graduates who create and guide the new technologies crucial to a postindustrial society.

In addition to the economic characteristics of a postindustrial society, changing values and norms reflect the changing influences on the society. Outsourcing of manufactured goods, for example, changes how members of a society see and treat foreigners or immigrants. Also, those individuals previously occupied in the manufacturing sector find themselves with no clearly defined social role.

There are a number of direct effects of postindustrialism on the community. For the first time, the term "community" is associated less with geographical proximity and more with scattered, but like-minded, individuals. Advances in telecommunications and the Internet mean that telecommuting becomes more common, placing people farther away from their place of work and their coworkers.

The relationship between manufacturing and services changes in a postindustrial society. Moving to a service-based economy means that manufacturing must occur elsewhere and is often outsourced (that is, sent away from a company to a contracted supplier) to industrial economies. While this gives the illusion that the postindustrial society is merely service-based, it is still highly connected with those industrial economies to which the manufacturing is outsourced.

## CHAPTER 5

# TECHNOLOGICAL ADVANCES OF THE INDUSTRIAL REVOLUTION

The Industrial Revolution has been a worldwide phenomenon, at least in so far as it has occurred in all those parts of the world, of which there are very few exceptions, where the influence of Western civilization has been felt. Beyond any doubt it occurred first in Britain, and its effects spread only gradually to continental Europe and North America. Equally clearly, the Industrial Revolution that eventually transformed these parts of the Western world surpassed in magnitude the achievements of Britain, and the process was carried further to change radically the socioeconomic life of Asia, Africa, Latin America, and Australasia. The reasons for this succession of events are complex, but they were implicit in the earlier account of the buildup toward rapid industrialization. Partly through good fortune and partly through conscious effort, Britain by the early 18th century came to possess the combination of social needs and social resources that provided the necessary preconditions of commercially successful innovation and a social system capable of sustaining and institutionalizing the processes of rapid technological change once they had started. This section will therefore be concerned, in the first place, with events in Britain, although in discussing later phases of the period it will be necessary to trace the way in which British technical achievements were diffused and superseded in other parts of the Western world.

# POWER TECHNOLOGY

An outstanding feature of the Industrial Revolution was the advance in power technology. At the beginning of this period, the major sources of power available to industry and any other potential consumer were animate energy and the power of wind and water, the only exception of any significance being the atmospheric steam engines that had been installed for pumping purposes, mainly in coal mines. It is to be emphasized that this use of steam power was exceptional and remained so for most industrial purposes until well into the 19th century. Steam did not simply replace other sources of power: it transformed them. The same sort of scientific inquiry that led to the development of the steam engine was also applied to the traditional sources of inanimate energy, with the result that both waterwheels and windmills were improved in design and efficiency. Numerous engineers contributed to the refinement of waterwheel construction, and by the middle of the 19th century new designs made possible increases in the speed of revolution of the waterwheel and thus prepared the way for the emergence of the water turbine, which is still an extremely efficient device for converting energy.

## STEAM ENGINES

Although the qualification regarding older sources of power is important, steam became the characteristic and ubiquitous power source of the British Industrial Revolution. Little development took place in the Newcomen atmospheric engine until James Watt patented a separate condenser in 1769, but from that point onward the steam engine underwent almost continuous improvements for more than a century. Watt's separate condenser was the outcome of his work on a model of a Newcomen engine that was being used in a University of Glasgow labouratory. Watt's inspiration was to separate the two actions of heating the cylinder with hot steam and cooling it to condense the steam for every stroke of the engine. By keeping the cylinder permanently hot and the condenser permanently cold, a great economy on energy used could be effected. This brilliantly simple idea could not be immediately incorporated in a full-scale engine because the engineering of such machines had hitherto been crude and defective. The backing of a Birmingham industrialist, Matthew Boulton, with his resources of capital and technical competence, was needed to convert the idea into a commercial success. Between 1775 and 1800, the period over which Watt's patents were extended, the Boulton and Watt partnership produced some 500 engines, which despite their high cost in relation to a Newcomen engine were eagerly acquired by the tin-mining industrialists of Cornwall and other power users who badly needed a more economic and reliable source of energy.

During the quarter of a century in which Boulton and Watt exercised their virtual monopoly over the manufacture of improved steam engines, they introduced many important refinements. Basically they converted the engine from a single-acting (i.e., applying power only on the downward stroke of the piston) atmospheric pumping machine into a versatile prime mover that was double-acting and could be applied to rotary motion, thus driving the wheels of industry. The rotary action engine was quickly adopted by British textile manufacturer Sir Richard Arkwright for use in a cotton mill, and although the ill-fated Albion Mill, at the southern end of Blackfriars Bridge in London, was burned down in 1791, when it had been in use for only five years and was still incomplete, it demonstrated the feasibility of applying steam power to large-scale grain milling. Many other industries followed in exploring the possibilities of steam power, and it soon became widely used.

Watt's patents had the temporary effect of restricting the development of high-pressure steam, necessary in such major power applications as the locomotive. This development came quickly once these patents lapsed in 1800. The Cornish engineer Richard Trevithick introduced higher steam pressures, achieving an unprecedented pressure of 145 pounds per square inch (10 kilograms per square centimetre) in 1802 with an experimental engine at Coalbrookdale, which worked safely and efficiently. Almost simultaneously, the versatile American engineer Oliver Evans built the first high-pressure steam engine in the United States, using, like Trevithick, a cylindrical boiler with an internal fire plate and flue. High-pressure steam engines rapidly became popular in America, partly as a result of Evans's initiative and partly because very few Watt-type low-pressure engines crossed the Atlantic. Trevithick quickly applied his engine to a vehicle, making the first successful steam locomotive for the Penydarren tramroad in South Wales in 1804. The success, however, was technological rather than commercial because the locomotive fractured the cast iron track of the tramway: the age of the railroad had to await further development both of the permanent way and of the locomotive.

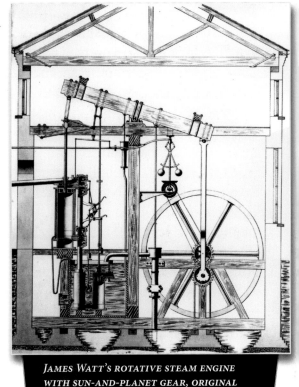

*JAMES WATT'S ROTATIVE STEAM ENGINE WITH SUN-AND-PLANET GEAR, ORIGINAL DRAWING, 1788. IN THE SCIENCE MUSEUM, LONDON.*

Meanwhile, the stationary steam engine advanced steadily to meet an ever-widening market of industrial requirements. High-pressure steam led to the development of the large beam pumping engines with a complex sequence of valve actions, which became universally known as Cornish engines; their distinctive characteristic was the cutoff of steam injection before the stroke was complete in order to allow the steam to do work by expanding. These engines were used all over the world for heavy pumping duties, often being shipped out and installed by Cornish engineers. Trevithick himself spent many years improving pumping engines in Latin America. Cornish engines, however, were probably most common in Cornwall itself, where they were used in large numbers in the tin and copper mining industries.

Another consequence of high-pressure steam was the practice of compounding, of using the steam twice or more at descending pressures before it was finally condensed or exhausted. The technique was first applied by Arthur Woolf, a Cornish mining engineer, who by 1811 had produced a very satisfactory and efficient compound beam engine with a high-pressure cylinder placed alongside the low-pressure cylinder, with both piston rods attached to the same pin of the parallel motion, which was a parallelogram of rods connecting the piston to the beam, patented by Watt in 1784. In 1845 John McNaught introduced an alternative form of compound beam engine, with the high-pressure cylinder on the opposite end of the beam from the low-pressure cylinder, and working with a shorter stroke. This became a very popular design. Various other methods of compounding steam engines were adopted, and the practice became increasingly widespread; in the second half of the 19th century triple- or quadruple-expansion engines were being used in industry and marine propulsion. By this time also the conventional beam-type vertical engine adopted by Newcomen and retained by Watt began to be replaced by horizontal-cylinder designs. Beam engines remained in use for some purposes until the eclipse of the reciprocating steam engine in the 20th century, and other types of vertical engine remained popular, but for both large and small duties the engine designs with horizontal cylinders became by far the most common.

A demand for power to generate electricity stimulated new thinking about the steam engine in the 1880s. Designers began to investigate the possibilities of radical modifications to the reciprocating engine to achieve the speeds desired, or of devising a steam engine working on a completely different principle. Full success in achieving a high-speed steam engine, however, depended on the steam turbine, a design of such novelty that it constituted a major technological innovation. This was invented by Sir Charles Parsons in 1884. By passing steam through the blades of a series of rotors of gradually increasing size (to allow for the expansion of the steam) the energy of the steam was converted to very rapid circular motion, which was ideal for generating electricity. Many refinements have since been made in turbine construction and the size of turbines has been vastly increased, but the basic principles remain the same, and this method still provides the main source of electric power except in those areas in which the mountainous terrain permits the economic generation of hydroelectric power by water turbines. Even the most modern nuclear power plants use steam turbines because technology has not yet solved the problem of transforming nuclear energy directly into electricity. In marine propulsion, too, the steam turbine remains an important source of power despite competition from the internal-combustion engine.

## ELECTRICITY

The development of electricity as a source of power preceded this conjunction with steam power late in the 19th century. The pioneering work had been done by an international collection of scientists including Benjamin Franklin of Pennsylvania, Alessandro Volta of the University of Pavia, Italy, and Michael

Faraday of Britain. It was the latter who had demonstrated the nature of the elusive relationship between electricity and magnetism in 1831, and his experiments provided the point of departure for both the mechanical generation of electric current, previously available only from chemical reactions within voltaic piles or batteries, and the utilization of such current in electric motors. Both the mechanical generator and the motor depend on the rotation of a continuous coil of conducting wire between the poles of a strong magnet: turning the coil produces a current in it, while passing a current through the coil causes it to turn. Both generators and motors underwent substantial development in the middle decades of the 19th century. In particular, French, German, Belgian, and Swiss engineers evolved the most satisfactory forms of armature (the coil of wire) and produced the dynamo, which made the large-scale generation of electricity commercially feasible.

The next problem was that of finding a market. In Britain, with its now well-established tradition of steam power, coal, and coal gas, such a market was not immediately obvious. But in continental Europe and North America there was more scope for experiment. In the United States Thomas Edison applied his inventive genius to finding fresh uses for electricity, and his development of the carbon-filament lamp showed how this form of energy could rival gas as a domestic illuminant. The problem had been that electricity had been used successfully for large installations such as lighthouses in which arc lamps had been powered by generators on the premises, but no way of subdividing the electric light into many small units had been devised. The principle of the filament lamp was that a thin conductor could be made incandescent by an electric current provided that it was sealed in a vacuum to keep it from burning out. Edison and the English chemist Sir Joseph Swan experimented with various materials for the filament and both chose carbon. The result was a highly successful small lamp, which could be varied in size for any sort of requirement. It is relevant that the success of the carbon-filament lamp did not immediately mean the supersession of gas lighting. Coal gas had first been used for lighting by William Murdock at his home in Redruth, Cornwall, where he was the agent for the Boulton and Watt company, in 1792. When he moved to the headquarters of the firm at Soho in Birmingham in 1798, Matthew Boulton authorized him to experiment in lighting the buildings there by gas, and gas lighting was subsequently adopted by firms and towns all over Britain in the first half of the 19th century. Lighting was normally provided by a fishtail jet of burning gas, but under the stimulus of competition from electric lighting the quality of gas lighting was greatly enhanced by the invention of the gas mantle. Thus improved, gas lighting remained popular for some forms of street lighting until the middle of the 20th century.

Lighting alone could not provide an economical market for electricity because its use was confined to the hours of darkness. Successful commercial generation depended upon the development of other uses for electricity, and particularly on electric traction. The popularity of urban electric tramways and the adoption of electric traction on subway systems such as the London Underground thus coincided with the widespread construction of generating equipment in the late 1880s and 1890s. The subsequent spread of this form of energy is one of the most remarkable technological success stories of the 20th century, but most of the basic techniques of generation, distribution, and utilization had been mastered by the end of the 19th century.

## INTERNAL-COMBUSTION ENGINE

Electricity does not constitute a prime mover, for however important it may be as a form of energy it has to be derived from a mechanical generator powered by water, steam, or internal combustion. The internal-combustion engine is a prime mover, and it emerged in the 19th century as a result both of greater scientific understanding of the principles of thermodynamics and of a search by engineers for a substitute for steam power in certain circumstances. In an internal-combustion engine the fuel is burned in the engine: the cannon provided an early model of a single-stroke engine; and several persons had experimented with gunpowder as a means of driving a piston in a cylinder. The major problem was that of finding a suitable fuel, and the secondary problem was that of igniting the fuel in an enclosed space to produce an action that could be easily and quickly repeated. The first problem was solved in the mid-19th century by the introduction of town gas supplies, but the second problem proved more intractable as it was difficult to maintain ignition evenly. The first successful gas engine was made by Étienne Lenoir in Paris in 1859. It was modeled closely on a horizontal steam engine, with an explosive mixture of gas and air ignited by an electric spark on alternate sides of the piston when it was in midstroke position. Although technically satisfactory, the engine was expensive to operate, and it was not until the refinement introduced by the German inventor Nikolaus Otto in 1878 that the gas engine became a commercial success. Otto adopted the four-stroke cycle of induction-compression-firing-exhaust that has been known by his name ever since. Gas engines became extensively used for small industrial establishments, which could thus dispense with the upkeep of a boiler necessary in any steam plant, however small.

## PETROLEUM

The economic potential for the internal-combustion engine lay in the need for a light locomotive engine. This could not be provided by the gas engine, depending on a piped supply of town gas, any more than by the steam engine, with its need for a cumbersome boiler; but, by using alternative fuels derived from oil, the internal-combustion engine took to wheels, with momentous consequences. Bituminous deposits had been known in Southwest Asia from antiquity and had been worked for building material, illuminants, and medicinal products. The westward expansion of settlement in America, with many homesteads beyond the range of city gas supplies, promoted the exploitation of the easily available sources of crude oil for the manufacture of kerosene (paraffin). In 1859 the oil industry took on new significance when Edwin L. Drake bored successfully through 69 feet (21 metres) of rock to strike oil in Pennsylvania, thus inaugurating the search for and exploitation of the deep oil resources of the world. While world supplies of oil expanded dramatically, the main demand was at first for the kerosene, the middle fraction distilled from the raw material, which was used as the fuel in oil lamps. The most volatile fraction of the oil, gasoline, remained an embarrassing waste product until it was discovered that this could be burned in a light internal-combustion engine; the result was an ideal prime mover for vehicles. The way was prepared for this development by the success of oil engines burning cruder fractions of oil. Kerosene-burning oil engines, modeled closely on existing gas engines, had emerged in the 1870s, and by the late 1880s engines using the vapour of heavy oil in a jet of compressed air and working on the Otto cycle had become an attractive proposition for light duties in places too isolated to use town gas.

The greatest refinements in the heavy-oil engine are associated with the work of Rudolf Diesel of Germany, who took out his first patents in 1892. Working from thermodynamic principles of minimizing heat losses, Diesel devised an engine in which the very high compression of the air in the cylinder secured the spontaneous ignition of the oil when it was injected in a carefully determined quantity. This ensured high thermal efficiency, but it also made necessary a heavy structure because of the high compression maintained, and also a rather rough performance at low speeds compared with other oil engines. It was therefore not immediately suitable for locomotive purposes, but Diesel went on improving his engine and in the 20th century it became an important form of vehicular propulsion.

Meantime the light high-speed gasoline (petrol) engine predominated. The first applications of the new engine to locomotion were made in Germany, where Gottlieb Daimler and Karl Benz equipped the first motorcycle and the first motorcar respectively with engines of their own design in 1885. Benz's "horseless carriage" became the prototype of the modern automobile, the development and consequences of which can be more conveniently considered in relation to the revolution in transport.

By the end of the 19th century, the internal-combustion engine was challenging the steam engine in many industrial and transport applications. It is notable that, whereas the pioneers of the steam engine had been almost all Britons, most of the innovators in internal combustion were continental Europeans and Americans. The transition, indeed, reflects the general change in international leadership in the Industrial Revolution, with Britain being gradually displaced from its position of unchallenged superiority in

Benz tricycle of 1886 - with Karl Benz at the controls.

*THE THREE-WHEELED BENZ MOTOR CAR, HERE DRIVEN BY BENZ, WAS THE PRECURSOR TO THE MODERN AUTOMOBILE.*

industrialization and technological innovation. A similar transition occurred in the theoretical understanding of heat engines: it was the work of the Frenchman Sadi Carnot and other scientific investigators that led to the new science of thermodynamics, rather than that of the British engineers who had most practical experience of the engines on which the science was based.

The transformation of power technology in the Industrial Revolution had repercussions throughout industry and society. In the first place, the demand for fuel stimulated the coal industry, which had already grown rapidly by the beginning of the 18th century, into continuing expansion and innovation. The steam engine, which enormously increased the need for coal, contributed significantly toward obtaining it by providing more efficient mine pumps and, eventually, improved ventilating equipment. Other inventions such as that of the miners' safety lamp helped to improve working conditions, although the immediate consequence of its introduction in 1816 was to persuade mineowners to work dangerous seams, which had thitherto been regarded as inaccessible. The principle of the lamp was that the flame from the wick of an oil lamp was enclosed within a cylinder of wire gauze, through which insufficient heat passed to ignite the explosive gas (firedamp) outside. It was subsequently improved but remained a vital source of light in coal mines until the advent of electric battery lamps. With these improvements, together with the simultaneous revolution in the transport system, British coal production increased steadily throughout the 19th century. The other important fuel for the new prime movers was petroleum, and the rapid expansion of its production has already been mentioned. In the hands of John D. Rockefeller and his Standard Oil organization it grew into a vast undertaking in the United States after the end of the Civil War, but the oil-extraction industry was not so well organized elsewhere until the 20th century.

## DEVELOPMENT OF INDUSTRIES

The innovations of the Industrial Revolution brought rise to several industries that became big business, both in Britain and elsewhere.

## METALLURGY

The development of techniques for working with iron and steel was one of the outstanding British achievements of the Industrial Revolution. The essential characteristic of this achievement was that changing the fuel of the iron and steel industry from charcoal to coal enormously increased the production of these metals. It also provided another incentive to coal production and made available the materials that were indispensable for the construction of steam engines and every other sophisticated form of machine. The transformation that began with a coke-smelting process in 1709 was carried further by the development of crucible steel in about 1740 and by the puddling and rolling process to produce wrought iron in 1784.

The result of this series of innovations was that the British iron and steel industry was freed from its reliance upon the forests as a source of charcoal and was encouraged to move toward the major coalfields. Abundant cheap iron thus became an outstanding feature of the early stages of the Industrial Revolution in Britain. Cast iron was available for bridge construction, for the framework of fireproof factories, and for other civil-engineering purposes such as Thomas Telford's novel cast-iron aqueducts. Wrought iron was available for all manner of mechanical devices requiring strength and precision. Steel remained a comparatively rare metal until the second half of the 19th century, when the situation was transformed by the Bessemer and Siemens processes for manufacturing steel in bulk. Henry Bessemer took out the patent for his converter in 1856. It consisted of a large vessel charged with molten iron, through which cold air was blown. There was a spectacular reaction resulting from the combination of impurities in the iron with oxygen in the air, and when this subsided it left mild steel in the converter. Meanwhile, the Siemens-Martin open-hearth process was introduced in 1864, utilizing the hot waste gases of cheap fuel to heat a regenerative furnace, with the initial heat transferred to the gases circulating round the large hearth in which the reactions within the molten metal could be carefully controlled to produce steel of the quality required. The open-hearth process was gradually refined and by the end of the 19th century had overtaken the Bessemer process in the amount of steel produced. The effect of these two processes was to make steel available in bulk instead of small-scale ingots of cast crucible steel, and thenceforward steel steadily replaced wrought iron as the major commodity of the iron and steel industry.

The transition to cheap steel did not take place without technical problems, one of the most difficult of which was the fact that most of the easily available low-grade iron ores in the world contain a proportion of phosphorus, which proved difficult to eliminate but which ruined any steel produced from them. The problem was solved by the British scientists S.G. Thomas and Percy Gilchrist, who invented the basic slag process, in which the furnace or converter was lined with an alkaline material with which the phosphorus could combine to produce a phosphatic slag; this, in turn, became an important raw material in the nascent artificial-fertilizer industry. The most important effect of this innovation was to make the extensive phosphoric ores of Lorraine and elsewhere available for exploitation. Among other things, therefore, it contributed significantly to the rise of the German heavy iron and steel industry in the Ruhr. Other improvements in British steel production were made in the late 19th century, particularly in the development of alloys for specialized purposes, but these contributed more to the quality than the quantity of steel and did not affect the shift away from Britain to continental Europe and

# HENRY BESSEMER

Henry Bessemer was born on Jan. 19, 1813, in Charlton, Hertfordshire, England. The son of an engineer, he demonstrated mechanical skill and the creativity of an inventor early in life.

One of Bessemer's early inventions was the changeable stamp for dating deeds and other government documents. Soon after this, he manufactured a "gold" powder made from brass for use in paints. The ornamental decorations of the time called for great quantities of such material. Bessemer's secret process soon brought him great wealth.

During the Crimean War, he invented an artillery shell that was too powerful for the cast-iron cannons being used by France. Upon learning of this problem, he attempted to produce a stronger cast iron. In his experiments Bessemer discovered that the excess oxygen in the hot gases of his furnace appeared to have removed the carbon from the pig iron that was being preheated, leaving a skin of pure iron. Bessemer then found that blowing air through melted cast iron not only purified the iron but also heated it further, allowing the purified iron to be easily poured. He was soon able to produce large, slag-free ingots that were highly workable. He invented the tilting converter into which molten pig iron could be poured before air was blown in from below.

His announcement of this process in 1856 brought many ironmasters to his door. Many licenses for using the process were granted. Very soon, however, it became clear that two elements harmful to iron, phosphorus and sulfur, were not removed by the process—at least not by the fireclay lining of Bessemer's converter. He had, unknown to himself, been using phosphorus-free iron, but the ironmasters were not so lucky. Bessemer was forced to call in his licenses and to find a phosphorus-free source of iron.

Once the phosphorus problem was solved, Bessemer became a licensor once again, and vast profits flowed in. It became clear

(*continued on the next page*)

**131**

## HENRY BESSEMER (CONTINUED)

that "mild steel"—as distinguished from the hard tool steels—could more reliably be used in place of wrought iron for ship plate, girders, rivets, and other items. This process, and later the invention in the late 1860s of the open-hearth process, have both yielded to oxygen steelmaking, a development of the Bessemer process.

In his later years Bessemer continued to make discoveries. He built a solar furnace, he designed and built an astronomical telescope, and he developed a set of machines for polishing diamonds. In addition to his knighthood, he received many honors. He died in London on March 15, 1898.

North America of dominance in this industry. British production continued to increase, but by 1900 it had been overtaken by that of the United States and Germany.

## MECHANICAL ENGINEERING

Closely linked with the iron and steel industry was the rise of mechanical engineering, brought about by the demand for steam engines and other large machines, and taking shape for the first time in the Soho workshop of Boulton and Watt in Birmingham, where the skills of the precision engineer, developed in manufacturing scientific instruments and small arms, were first applied to the construction of large industrial machinery. The engineering workshops that matured in the 19th century played a vital part in the increasing mechanization of industry and transport. Not only did they deliver the looms, locomotives, and other hardware in steadily growing quantities, but they also transformed the machine tools on which these machines were made. The lathe became an all-metal, power-driven machine with a completely rigid base and a slide rest to hold the cutting tool, capable of more sustained and vastly more accurate work than the hand- or foot-operated wooden-framed lathes that preceded it. Drilling and slotting machines, milling and planing machines, and a steam hammer invented by James Nasmyth (an inverted vertical steam engine with the hammer on the lower end of the piston rod), were among the machines devised or improved from earlier woodworking models by the new mechanical engineering industry. After the middle of the 19th century, specialization within the machinery industry became more pronounced, as some manufacturers concentrated on vehicle production while others devoted themselves to the particular needs of industries such as coal mining, papermaking, and sugar refining. This movement toward greater specialization was accelerated by the establishment of mechanical engineering in the other industrial nations, especially in Germany, where electrical engineering and other new skills made rapid progress, and in the United States, where labour shortages encouraged the development of standardization and mass-production techniques in fields as widely separated as agricultural machinery, small arms, typewriters, and sewing machines. Even before the coming of the bicycle, the automobile, and the airplane, therefore, the pattern of the modern engineering industry had been clearly established. The dramatic increases in engineering precision, represented by the machine designed by British mechanical engineer Sir Joseph Whitworth in 1856 for measuring to an accuracy of 0.000001 inch (even though such refinement was not necessary in everyday workshop practice), and the corresponding increase in the productive capacity of the engineering industry, acted as a continuing encouragement to further mechanical innovation.

# THE INDUSTRIAL REVOLUTION
## STEAM AND STEEL

## TEXTILES

The industry that, probably more than any other, gave its character to the British Industrial Revolution was the cotton-textile industry. The traditional dates of the Industrial Revolution bracket the period in which the processes of cotton manufacture in Britain were transformed from those of a small-scale domestic industry scattered over the towns and villages of the South Pennines into those of a large-scale, concentrated, power-driven, mechanized,

THIS ARTIST'S RENDERING SHOWS JAMES NASMYTH'S STEAM HAMMER.

factory-organized, urban industry. The transformation was undoubtedly dramatic both to contemporaries and to posterity, and there is no doubting its immense significance in the overall pattern of British industrialization. But its importance in the history of technology should not be exaggerated. Certainly there were many interesting mechanical improvements, at least at the beginning of the transformation. The development of the spinning wheel into the spinning jenny, and the use of rollers and moving trolleys to mechanize spinning in the shape of the frame and the mule, respectively, initiated a drastic rise in the productivity of the industry. But these were secondary innovations in the sense that there were precedents for them in the experiments of the previous generation; that in any case the first British textile factory was the Derby silk mill built in 1719; and that the most far-reaching innovation in cotton manufacture was the introduction of steam power to drive carding machines, spinning machines, power looms, and printing machines. This, however, is probably to overstate the case, and the cotton innovators should not be deprived of credit for their enterprise and ingenuity in transforming the British cotton industry and making it the model for subsequent exercises in industrialization. Not only was it copied, belatedly and slowly, by the woolen-cloth industry in Britain, but wherever other nations sought to industrialize they tried to acquire British cotton machinery and the expertise of British cotton industrialists and artisans.

One of the important consequences of the rapid rise of the British cotton industry was the dynamic stimulus it gave to other processes and industries. The rising demand for raw cotton, for example, encouraged the plantation economy of the southern United States and the introduction of the cotton gin, an important contrivance for separating mechanically the cotton fibres from the seeds, husks, and stems of the plant.

## CHEMICALS

In Britain the growth of the textile industry brought a sudden increase of interest in the chemical industry because one formidable bottleneck in the production of textiles was the long time that was taken by natural bleaching techniques, relying on sunlight, rain, sour milk, and urine. The modern chemical industry was virtually called into being in order to develop more rapid bleaching techniques for the British

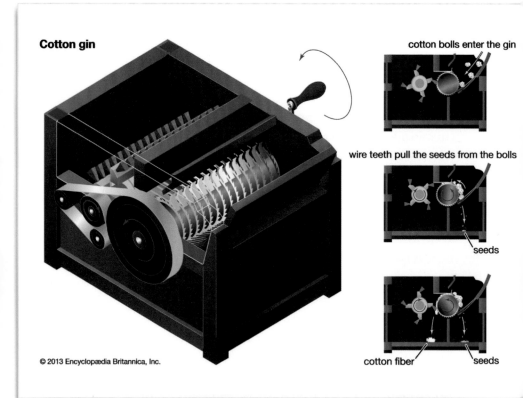

Cotton gin

cotton bolls enter the gin

wire teeth pull the seeds from the bolls

seeds

cotton fiber          seeds

© 2013 Encyclopædia Britannica, Inc.

*A DIAGRAM OF A COTTON GIN SHOWS HOW THE MACHINE SEPARATES THE SEEDS FROM THE COTTON FIBER.*

cotton industry. Its first success came in the middle of the 18th century, when John Roebuck invented the method of mass producing sulfuric acid in lead chambers. The acid was used directly in bleaching, but it was also used in the production of more effective chlorine bleaches, and in the manufacture of bleaching powder, a process perfected by Charles Tennant at his St. Rollox factory in Glasgow in 1799. This product effectively met the requirements of the cotton-textile industry, and thereafter the chemical industry turned its attention to the needs of other industries, and particularly to the increasing demand for alkali in soap, glass, and a range of other manufacturing processes. The result was the successful establishment of the Leblanc soda process, patented by Nicolas Leblanc in France in 1791, for manufacturing sodium carbonate (soda) on a large scale; this remained the main alkali process used in Britain until the end of the 19th century, even though the Belgian Solvay process, which was considerably more economical, was replacing it elsewhere.

Innovation in the chemical industry shifted, in the middle of the 19th century, from the heavy chemical processes to organic chemistry. The stimulus here was less a specific industrial demand than the pioneering work of a group of German scientists on the nature of coal and its derivatives. Following their work, W.H. Perkin, at the Royal College of Chemistry in London, produced the first artificial dye from aniline in 1856. In the same period, the middle third of the 19th century, work on the qualities of cellulosic materials was leading to the development of high explosives such as nitrocellulose, nitroglycerine, and dynamite, while experiments with the solidification and extrusion of cellulosic liquids were producing the first plastics, such as celluloid, and the first artificial fibres, so-called artificial silk, or rayon. By the end of the century all these processes had become the bases for large chemical industries.

An important by-product of the expanding chemical industry was the manufacture of a widening range of medicinal and pharmaceutical materials as medical knowledge increased and drugs began to play a constructive part in therapy. The period of the Industrial Revolution witnessed the first real progress in medical services since the ancient civilizations. Great advances in the sciences of anatomy and physiology had had remarkably little effect on medical practice. In 18th-century Britain, however, hospital provision increased in quantity although not invariably in quality, while a significant start was made in immunizing people against smallpox culminating in Edward Jenner's vaccination process of 1796, by which protection from the disease was provided by administering a dose of the much less virulent but related disease of cowpox. But it took many decades of use and further smallpox epidemics to secure its widespread adoption and thus to make it effective in controlling the disease. By this time Louis Pasteur and others had established the bacteriological origin of many common diseases and thereby helped to promote movements for better public health and immunization against many virulent diseases such as typhoid fever and diphtheria. Parallel improvements in anesthetics (beginning with Sir Humphry Davy's discovery of nitrous oxide, or "laughing gas," in 1799) and antiseptics were making possible elabourate surgery, and by the end of the century X-rays and radiology were placing powerful new tools at the disposal of medical technology, while the use of synthetic drugs such as the barbiturates and aspirin (acetylsalicylic acid) had become established.

## AGRICULTURE

The agricultural improvements of the 18th century had been promoted by people whose industrial and commercial interests made them willing to experiment with new machines and processes to improve the productivity of their estates. Under the same sort of stimuli, agricultural improvement continued into the 19th century and was extended to food processing in Britain and elsewhere. The steam engine was not readily adapted for agricultural purposes, yet ways were found of harnessing it to threshing machines and even to plows by means of a cable between powerful traction engines pulling a plow across a field. In the United States mechanization of agriculture began later than in Britain, but because of the comparative labour shortage it proceeded more quickly and more thoroughly. The McCormick reaper and the combine harvester were both developed in the United States, as were barbed wire and the food-packing and canning industries, Chicago becoming the centre for these processes. The introduction of refrigeration techniques in the second half of the 19th century made it possible to convey meat from Australia and Argentina to European markets, and the same markets encouraged the growth of dairy farming and market gardening, with distant producers such as New Zealand able to send their butter in refrigerated ships to wherever in the world it could be sold.

THE INDUSTRIAL REVOLUTION

## CIVIL ENGINEERING

For large civil-engineering works, the heavy work of moving earth continued to depend throughout this period on human labour organized by building contractors. But the use of gunpowder, dynamite, and steam diggers helped to reduce this dependence toward the end of the 19th century, and the introduction of compressed air and hydraulic tools also contributed to the lightening of drudgery. The latter two inventions were important in other respects, such as in mining engineering and in the operation of lifts, lock gates, and cranes. The use of a tunneling shield, to allow a tunnel to be driven through soft or uncertain rock strata, was pioneered by the French émigré engineer Marc Brunel in the construction of the first tunnel underneath the Thames River in London (1825–42), and the technique was adopted elsewhere. The iron bell or caisson was introduced for working below water level in order to lay foundations for bridges or other structures, and bridge building made great advances with the perfecting of the suspension bridge—by the British engineers Thomas Telford and Isambard Kingdom Brunel and the German American engineer John Roebling—and the development of the truss bridge, first in timber, then in iron. Wrought iron gradually replaced cast iron as a bridge-building material, although several distinguished cast-iron bridges survive, such as that erected at Ironbridge in Shropshire between 1777 and 1779, which has been fittingly described as the "Stonehenge of the Industrial Revolution." The sections were cast at the Coalbrookdale furnace nearby and assembled by mortising and wedging on the model of a timber construction, without the use of bolts or rivets. The design was quickly superseded in other cast-iron bridges, but the bridge still stands as the first important structural use of cast iron. Cast iron became very important in the framing of large buildings, the elegant Crystal Palace of 1851 being an outstanding example. This was designed by the ingenious gardener-turned-architect Sir Joseph Paxton on the model of a greenhouse that he had built on the Chatsworth estate of the duke of Devonshire. Its cast-iron beams were manufactured by three different firms and tested for size and strength on the site. By the end of the 19th century, however, steel was beginning to replace cast iron as well as wrought iron, and reinforced concrete was being introduced. In water-supply and sewage-disposal works, civil engineering achieved some monumental successes, especially in the design of dams, which improved considerably in the period, and in long-distance piping and pumping.

## TRANSPORT

Transport provides an example of a revolution within the Industrial Revolution, so completely was it transformed in the period 1750–1900. The first improvements in Britain came in roads and canals in the second half of the 18th century. Good roads and canals had existed in continental Europe for at least a century before their adoption in Britain; nevertheless, by the beginning of the 19th century, British engineers were beginning to innovate in both road- and canal-building techniques, with J.L. McAdam's inexpensive and long-wearing road surface of compacted stones and Thomas Telford's well-engineered canals. The outstanding innovation in transport, however, was the application of steam power, which occurred in three forms.

First was the evolution of the railroad: the combination of the steam locomotive and a permanent travel way of metal rails. Experiments in this conjunction in the first quarter of the 19th century culminated in the Stockton & Darlington Railway, opened in 1825, and a further five years of experience with steam locomotives led to the Liverpool and Manchester Railway, which, when it opened in 1830, constituted the first fully timetabled railway service with scheduled freight and passenger traffic relying entirely on the steam locomotive for traction. This railway was designed by George Stephenson, and the locomotives were the work of Stephenson and his son Robert, the first locomotive being the famous *Rocket*, which won a competition held by the proprietors of the railway at Rainhill, outside Liverpool, in 1829. The opening of the Liverpool and Manchester line may fairly be regarded as the inauguration of the railway era, which continued until World War I. During this time railways were built across all the countries and continents of the world, opening up vast areas to the markets of industrial society. Locomotives increased rapidly in size and power, but the essential principles remained the same as those established by the Stephensons in the early 1830s: horizontal cylinders mounted beneath a multitubular boiler with a firebox at the rear and a tender carrying supplies of water and fuel. This was the form developed from the *Rocket*, which had diagonal cylinders, being itself a stage in the transition from the vertical cylinders, often encased by the boiler, which had been typical of the earliest locomotives (except Trevithick's Penydarren engine, which had a horizontal cylinder). Meanwhile, the construction of the permanent way underwent a corresponding improvement on that which had been common on the preceding tramroads: wrought-iron, and eventually steel, rails replaced the cast-iron rails, which cracked easily under a steam locomotive, and well-aligned track with easy gradients and substantial supporting civil-engineering works became a commonplace of the railroads of the world.

The second form in which steam power was applied to transport was that of the road locomotive. There is no technical reason why this should not have enjoyed a success equal to that of the railway engine, but its development was so constricted by the unsuitability of most roads and by the jealousy of other

THE "ROCKET," 1829.

*THE ROCKET WAS A LOCOMOTIVE BUILT BY GEORGE STEPHENSON.*

road users that it achieved general utility only for heavy traction work and such duties as road rolling. The steam traction engine, which could be readily adapted from road haulage to power farm machines, was nevertheless a distinguished product of 19th-century steam technology.

The third application was considerably more important because it transformed marine transport. The initial attempts to use a steam engine to power a boat were made on the Seine River in France in 1775, and several experimental steamships were built by William Symington in Britain at the turn of the 19th century. The first commercial success in steam propulsion for a ship, however, was that of the American Robert Fulton, whose paddle steamer the "North River Steamboat," commonly known as the *Clermont* after its first overnight port, plied between New York and Albany in 1807, equipped with a Boulton and Watt engine of the modified beam or side-lever type, with two beams placed alongside the base of the engine in order to lower the centre of gravity. A similar engine was installed in the Glasgow-built *Comet*, which was put in service on the Clyde in 1812 and was the first successful steamship in Europe. All the early steamships were paddle-driven, and all were small vessels suitable only for ferry and packet duties because it was long thought that the fuel requirements of a steamship would be so large as to preclude long-distance cargo carrying. The further development of the steamship was thus delayed until the 1830s, when I.K. Brunel began to apply his ingenious and innovating mind to the problems of steamship construction. His three great steamships each marked a leap forward in technique. The *Great Western* (launched 1837), the first built specifically for oceanic service in the North Atlantic, demonstrated that the proportion of space required for fuel decreased as the total volume of the ship increased. The *Great Britain* (launched 1843) was the first

# GEORGE STEPHENSON

George Stephenson (1781–1848) was the son of a mechanic who operated a Newcomen atmospheric-steam engine that was used to pump out a coal mine at Newcastle upon Tyne. The boy went to work at an early age and without formal schooling; by age 19 he was operating a Newcomen engine.

In 1813 George Stephenson built the *Blucher*, an engine that drew eight loaded wagons carrying 30 tons of coal at 4 miles (6 km) per hour. Not satisfied, he sought to improve his locomotive's power and introduced the "steam blast," by which exhaust steam was redirected up the chimney, pulling air after it and increasing the draft. The new design made the locomotive truly practical.

Over the next few years, Stephenson built several locomotives and gained a measure of fame by inventing a mine-safety lamp. In 1821 he was commissioned to build a steam locomotive. On Sept. 27, 1825, railroad transportation was born when the first public passenger train, pulled by Stephenson's *Active* (later renamed *Locomotion*), ran from Darlington to Stockton, carrying 450 persons at 15 miles (24 km) per hour. Liverpool and Manchester interests called him in to build a 40-mile (64-kilometre) railroad line to connect the two cities. To survey and construct the line, Stephenson had to outwit the violent hostility of farmers and landlords who feared, among other things, that the railroad would supplant horse-drawn transportation and shut off the market for oats.

When the Liverpool-Manchester line was nearing completion in 1829, a competition was held for locomotives; Stephenson's new engine, the *Rocket*, which he built with his son, Robert, won with a speed of 36 miles (58 km) per hour. Eight locomotives were used when the Liverpool-Manchester line opened on Sept. 15, 1830, and all of them had been built in Stephenson's Newcastle works. From

## GEORGE STEPHENSON (CONTINUED)

this time on, railroad building spread rapidly throughout Britain, Europe, and North America, and George Stephenson continued as the chief guide of the revolutionary transportation medium, solving problems of roadway construction, bridge design, and locomotive and rolling-stock manufacture. He built many other railways in the Midlands, and he acted as consultant on many railroad projects at home and abroad.

large iron ship in the world and the first to be screw-propelled; its return to the port of Bristol in 1970, after a long working life and abandonment to the elements, is a remarkable testimony to the strength of its construction. The *Great Eastern* (launched 1858), with its total displacement of 18,918 tons, was by far the largest ship built in the 19th century. With a double iron hull and two sets of engines driving both a screw and paddles, this leviathan was never an economic success, but it admirably demonstrated the technical possibilities of the large iron steamship. By the end of the century, steamships were well on the way to displacing the sailing ship on all the main trade routes of the world.

## COMMUNICATIONS

Communications were equally transformed in the 19th century. The steam engine helped to mechanize and thus to speed up the processes of papermaking and printing. In the latter case the acceleration was achieved by the introduction of the high-speed rotary press and the Linotype machine for casting type and setting it in justified lines (i.e., with even right-hand

*ROBERT FULTON'S FIRST STEAMBOAT, LATER CALLED THE CLERMONT, MAKES ITS FIRST VOYAGE, FROM NEW YORK CITY TO ALBANY, NEW YORK, ON THE HUDSON RIVER, IN 1807.*

margins). Printing, indeed, had to undergo a technological revolution comparable to the 15th-century invention of movable type to be able to supply the greatly increasing market for the printed word. Another important process that was to make a vital contribution to modern printing was discovered and developed in the 19th century: photography. The first photograph was taken in 1826 or 1827 by the French physicist J.N. Niépce, using a pewter plate coated with a form of bitumen that hardened on exposure. His partner L.-J.-M. Daguerre and the Englishman W.H. Fox Talbot adopted silver compounds to give light sensitivity, and the technique developed rapidly in the middle decades of the century. By the 1890s George Eastman in the United States was manufacturing cameras and celluloid photographic film for a popular market, and the

**147**

*ALEXANDER GRAHAM BELL DEMONSTRATING THE ABILITY OF THE TELEPHONE TO TRANSMIT SOUND BY ELECTRICITY FROM SALEM TO BOSTON, MASSACHUSETTS, 1887.*

first experiments with the cinema were beginning to attract attention.

The great innovations in communications technology, however, derived from electricity. The first was the electric telegraph, invented or at least made into a practical proposition for use on the developing British railway system by two British inventors, Sir William Cooke and Sir Charles Wheatstone, who collabourated on the work and took out a joint patent in 1837. Almost simultaneously, the American inventor Samuel F.B. Morse devised the signaling code that was subsequently adopted

# ALEXANDER GRAHAM BELL

Alexander Graham Bell was born in Edinburgh, Scotland, on March 3, 1847. He was educated at Edinburgh University and University College, London. With his parents, he moved to Brantford, Ont., in 1870. His father and grandfather had devoted their lives to the study of human speech and to teaching the deaf to speak, and he followed their profession. His main interest throughout his life was in helping the deaf.

In 1871 Bell started teaching deaf pupils in Boston. The following year he opened a private school to train teachers of the deaf in the methods of visible speech, which had been devised by his father. He began teaching at Boston University in 1873. In July 1877 he married Mabel Hubbard, one of his pupils.

In 1874–75 he began work on his great invention, inspired by experiments with devices to help the deaf. On March 10, 1876, in Boston, the first sentence was successfully transmitted by telephone. The historic words were spoken to his assistant, Thomas Watson: "Mr. Watson, come here; I want you."

Bell's attorney had applied for a patent on February 14 of that year, just two hours before Elisha Gray filed a notice in the Patent Office covering some of the same principles. At the Centennial Exposition of 1876, in Philadelphia, Pa., the demonstrations of Bell's remarkable telephone made a great sensation among the general public. Bell helped found the magazine *Science* in 1880.

In 1880 Bell received the French government's Volta prize of 50,000 francs for his invention of the telephone. He used the money to establish the Volta Labouratory and the American Association to Promote the Teaching of Speech to the Deaf in Washington, D.C. The association's name was changed to the Alexander Graham Bell Association for the Deaf in 1956. It is an international information center for the oral education of the deaf.

(*continued on the next page*)

## ALEXANDER GRAHAM BELL (CONTINUED)

In 1898 Bell succeeded his father-in-law as president of the National Geographic Society. Convinced that geography could be taught through pictures, Bell sought to promote an understanding of life in distant lands in an era when only the privileged could travel. He was aided by his future son-in-law, Gilbert Grosvenor, who transformed what had begun as a modest pamphlet into a unique educational journal—*National Geographic* magazine.

Among Bell's other inventions was an audiometer, for measuring the intensity of sound. He also experimented in aviation. His wife founded the Aerial Experiment Association—the first research organization established by a woman.

For many years Bell spent his summers at his estate on Cape Breton Island in Nova Scotia. He died there on Aug. 2, 1922. During the funeral service every telephone of the Bell system was kept silent. In 1950 Bell was elected to the Hall of Fame at New York University.

all over the world. In the next quarter of a century the continents of the world were linked telegraphically by transoceanic cables, and the main political and commercial centres were brought into instantaneous communication. The telegraph system also played an important part in the opening up of the American West by providing rapid aid in the maintenance of law and order. The electric telegraph was followed by the telephone, invented by Alexander Graham Bell in 1876 and adopted quickly for short-range oral communication in the cities of America and at a somewhat more leisurely pace in those of Europe. About the same time, theoretical work on the electromagnetic properties of light and other radiation was beginning to produce astonishing experimental results, and the possibilities of wireless telegraphy began to be explored. By the end of the century, Guglielmo Marconi had transmitted messages over many miles in Britain and was preparing the apparatus with which he made the first transatlantic radio communication on Dec. 12, 1901. The world was thus being drawn inexorably into a closer community by the spread of instantaneous communication.

# A TECHNOLOGICAL AWARENESS

In the course of its dynamic development between 1750 and 1900, important things happened to technology. In the first place, it became self-conscious. This change is sometimes characterized as one from a craft-based technology to one based on science, but this is an oversimplification. What occurred was rather an increase in the awareness of technology as a socially important function. It is apparent in the growing volume of treatises on technological subjects from the 16th century onward and in the rapid development of patent legislation to protect the interests of technological innovators. It is apparent also in the development of technical education, uneven at first, being confined to the French polytechnics and spreading thence to Germany and North America but reaching even Britain, which had been most opposed to its formal recognition as part of the structure of education, by the end of the 19th century. Again, it is apparent in the growth of professional associations for engineers and for other specialized groups of technologists.

Second, by becoming self-conscious, technology attracted attention in a way it had never done before, and vociferous factions grew up to praise it as the mainspring of social progress and the development of democracy or to criticize it as the bane of modern man, responsible for the harsh discipline of the "dark Satanic mills" and the tyranny of the machine and the squalor of urban life. It was clear by the end of the 19th century that technology was an important feature in industrial society and that it was likely to become more so. Whatever was to happen in the future, technology had come of age and had to be taken seriously as a formative factor of the utmost significance in the continuing development of civilization.

# CONCLUSION

How or why some agrarian societies have evolved into industrial states is not always fully understood. What is certainly known, though, is that the changes that took place in Britain during the Industrial Revolution of the late 18th and 19th centuries provided a prototype for the early industrializing nations of western Europe and North America. Along with its technological components (e.g., the mechanization of labour and the reliance upon inanimate sources of energy), the process of industrialization entailed profound social developments. The freeing of the labourer from feudal and customary obligations created a free market in labour, with a pivotal role for a specific social type, the entrepreneur. Cities drew large numbers of people off the land, massing workers in the new industrial towns and factories.

Later industrializers attempted to manipulate some of these elements. The Soviet Union, for instance, industrialized largely on the basis of forced labour and eliminated the entrepreneur, while in Japan strong state involvement stimulated and sustained the entrepreneur's role. Other states, notably Denmark and New Zealand, industrialized primarily by commercializing and mechanizing agriculture.

Although urban-industrial life offers unprecedented opportunites for individual mobility and personal freedom, it can exact high social and psychological tolls. Such various observers as Karl Marx and Émile Durkheim cited the "alienation" and "anomie" of individual workers faced by seemingly meaningless tasks and rapidly altering goals. The fragmentation of the extended family and community tended to isolate individuals and to countervail traditional values. By the very mechanism of growth, industrialism appears to create a new strain of poverty, whose victims for a variety of reasons are unable to compete according to the rules of the industrial order. In the major industrialized nations of the late 20th century, such developments as automated technology, an expanding service sector, and increasing suburbanization signaled what some observers called the emergence of a postindustrial society.

# GLOSSARY

**ASSEMBLY LINE** Industrial arrangement of machines, equipment, and workers for continuous flow of workpieces in mass-production operations.

**BOURGEOISIE** The middle class.

**BURGHER** An inhabitant of a borough or a town.

**CAISSON** A watertight chamber used in construction work underwater or as a foundation.

**CAPITALISM** An economic system in which natural resources and means of production are privately owned, investments are determined by private decision rather than by state control, and prices, production, and the distribution of goods are determined mainly by competition in a free market.

**COLLIERY** A coal mine and the buildings connected with it.

**COTTAGE INDUSTRY** A system for making products to sell in which people work in their own homes and use their own equipment.

**ENLIGHTENMENT** A European intellectual movement of the 17th and 18th centuries in which ideas concerning God, reason, nature, and man were synthesized into a worldview that gained wide assent and that instigated revolutionary developments in art, philosophy, and politics.

**FEUDALISM** A system of political organization in medieval Europe in which a vassal gave service to a lord and received protection and land in return.

**FLYWHEEL** Heavy wheel attached to a rotating shaft so as to smooth out delivery of power from a motor to a machine. The inertia of the flywheel opposes and moderates fluctuations in the speed of the engine and stores the excess energy for intermittent use.

**GUILD**  A medieval association of merchants or craftsmen.

**INCANDESCENT LAMP**  Device that produces light by heating a suitable material to a high temperature. When any solid or gas is heated, commonly by combustion or resistance to an electric current, it gives off light of a colour (spectral balance) characteristic of the material.

**INDUSTRIAL REVOLUTION**  A rapid major change in an economy marked by the general introduction of power-driven machinery or by an important change in the prevailing types and methods of use of such machines.

**LABOUR**  The services performed by workers for wages as distinguished from those rendered by entrepreneurs for profits.

**LAISSEZ-FAIRE**  A doctrine opposing governmental interference in economic affairs beyond the minimum necessary for the maintenance of peace and property rights.

**LATHE**  A machine in which a piece of material is held and turned while being shaped by a tool.

**LINOTYPE**  Used for a typesetting machine that produces each line of type in the form of a solid metal slug.

**MERCANTILISM**  An economic system developing during the 17th and 18th centuries to unify and increase the power and wealth of a nation by strict governmental regulation of the economy usually through policies designed to secure an accumulation of bullion, a favorable balance of trade, the development of agriculture and manufactures, and the establishment of foreign trading monopolies.

**PATRON**  A person chosen as a special guardian or supporter.

**POSTINDUSTRIALIST SOCIETY**   A society marked by a transition from a manufacturing-based economy to a service-based economy, a transition that is also connected with subsequent societal restructuring.

**PRODUCTION** The making of goods available for human wants.

**PROTOTYPE** An original model on which something is patterned.

**RAISON D'ÊTRE** The reason for which a person or organization exists.

**SERFDOM** A condition in medieval Europe in which a tenant farmer was bound to a hereditary plot of land and to the will of his landlord.

**SERVICE INDUSTRY** An industry in which part of the economy creates services rather than tangible objects.

**SOVEREIGN** A monarch exercising supreme authority.

**SYNDICALISM** A system of economic organization in which industries are owned and managed by the workers.

**TELEGRAPH** An apparatus, system, or process for communication at a distance by electric transmission of such signals over wire.

# BIBLIOGRAPHY

## REVOLUTION AND THE GROWTH OF INDUSTRIAL SOCIETY, 1789-1914

Robin W. Winks and Thomas Kaiser, *Europe, 1648-1815: From the Old Regime to the Age of Revolution* (2004); T.C.W. Blanning (ed.), *The Nineteenth Century: Europe, 1789-1914* (2000); and Theodore S. Hamerow, *The Birth of a New Europe: State and Society in the Nineteenth Century* (1983), provide excellent introductions to the period. Comprehensive coverage is offered in E.J. Hobsbawm, *The Age of Revolution, 1789-1848* (1962), *The Age of Capital, 1848-1875* (1975, reissued 1984), and *The Age of Empire, 1875-1914* (1987). Treatments of the Industrial Revolution and related social developments include Lenard R. Berlanstein (ed.), *The Industrial Revolution and Work in Nineteenth-Century Europe* (1992); Phyllis Deane, *The First Industrial Revolution*, 2nd ed. (1979), an economic history; David S. Landes, *The Unbound Prometheus: Technological Change and Industrial Development in Western Europe from 1750 to the Present* (1969), more comprehensive and less quantitative, on society; Peter N. Stearns, *European Society in Upheaval: Social History Since 1750*, 2nd ed. (1975); Sidney Pollard, *Peaceful Conquest: The Industrialization of Europe, 1760-1970* (1981); and William L. Blackwell, *The Industrialization of Russia: An Historical Perspective*, 2nd ed. (1982).

Patterns of revolution are the subject of R.R. Palmer, *The Age of the Democratic Revolution: A Political History of Europe and America, 1760-1800*, 2 vol. (1959-64, reprinted 1974); Owen Connelly, *French Revolution, Napoleonic Era* (1979); and Lynn Hunt, *Politics, Culture, and Class in the French Revolution* (1984). Developments at mid-century are studied in Peter N. Stearns, *1848: The Revolutionary Tide in Europe* (1974); and Robin W. Winks and Joan Neuberger, *Europe and the Making of Modernity, 1815–1914* (2005). Political trends can be followed in several excellent national histories, including Gordon Wright, *France in Modern Times: From the Enlightenment to the Present*, 4th ed. (1987); Gordon A. Craig, *Germany, 1866–1945* (1978); and Asa Briggs, *The Making of Modern England, 1783–1867* (1965). Albert S. Lindemann, *A History of European Socialism* (1983), examines the vital political trend. Overviews of imperialism can be found in Toni Smith, *The Pattern of Imperialism: The United States, Great Britain, and the Late-Industrializing World Since 1815* (1981); and Winfried Baumgart, *Imperialism: The Idea and Reality of British and French Colonial Expansion*, 1880–1914, rev. ed. (1982; originally published in German, 1975). A.J.P. Taylor, *The Struggle for Mastery in Europe*, 1848–1918 (1954, reprinted 1971); and Arno J. Mayer, *The Persistence of the Old Regime: Europe to the Great War* (1981), interpret internal European diplomatic patterns. Readable accounts of the origins of the First World War include Laurence Lafore, *The Long Fuse: An Interpretation of the Origins of World War I*, 2nd ed. (1971); Barbara W. Tuchman, *The Proud Tower: A Portrait of the World Before the War, 1890–1914* (1966); and James Joll, *The Origins of the First World War* (1984). The studies by Fritz Fischer are crucial: *Germany's Aims in the First World War* (1967; originally published in German, 1961), and *The War of Illusions* (1975; originally published in German, 1969).

The historical role of Romanticism and Realism in philosophical, cultural, social, and political thought and the development of the modern culture of which they were the precursors is the focus of Eugen Weber, *Paths to the*

*Present: Aspects of European Thought from Romanticism to Existentialism* (1960); Harold T. Parker, *The Cult of Antiquity and the French Revolutionaries: A Study in the Development of the Revolutionary Spirit* (1937, reprinted 1965); Crane Brinton, *The Political Ideas of the English Romanticists* (1962); Jacques Barzun, *Classic, Romantic, and Modern*, 2nd rev. ed. (1975); and Nicholas Roe (ed.), *Romanticism: An Oxford Guide* (2005). Frederic Ewen, *Heroic Imagination: The Creative Genius of Europe from Waterloo (1815) to the Revolution of 1848* (1984), gives a broad summary with interpretive detail. Ernst Behler (ed.), *Philosophy of German Idealism* (1987), supplies both a review of common traits and comparative evaluations. Kenneth R. Johnston and Gene W. Ruoff (eds.), *The Age of William Wordsworth: Critical Essays on the Romantic Tradition* (1987), offers contrasting views on Romantic literature to 1850. Robert C. Binkley, *Realism and Nationalism: 1852–1871* (1935, reprinted 1963); and Carlton J.H. Hayes, *A Generation of Materialism, 1871–1900* (1941, reprinted 1983), add to the understanding of political and economic characteristics of the period and interpret its culture. William W. Stowe, *Balzac, James, and the Realistic Novel* (1983), considers the development of the genre from its inception to its modern transformations.

Bruce Bernard (ed.), *The Impressionist Revolution* (1986), interprets the broadest aspects of artistic innovation. Maly Gerhardus and Dietfried Gerhardus, *Symbolism and Art Nouveau: Sense of Impending Crisis, Refinement of Sensibility, and Life Reborn in Beauty* (1979; originally published in German, 1977), covers the last two decades of the 19th century in this excellently illustrated volume. Yvonne Brunhammer, *The Art Deco Style* (1983), examines the radical change in design characteristic of the new century. Lewis Mumford et al., *The Arts in Renewal* (1951, reprinted 1969), is a collection of interpretive studies on the historical establishment of modernism in various artistic genres. Henry R. Hitchcock, *Modern Architecture: Romanticism and Reintegration* (1929, reprinted 1972), offers a prospect and retrospect after a generation of the "International Style."

# THE HISTORY OF TECHNOLOGY

The best general work is still Charles Singer et al. (eds.), *A History of Technology*, 5 vol. (1954–58, reprinted 1957–65), extended by Trevor I. Williams (ed.), with 2 vol. (1978) on the 20th century. The single-volume companion studies, T.K. Derry and Trevor I. Williams, *A Short History of Technology from the Earliest Times to A.D. 1900* (1960, reissued 1970); and Trevor I. Williams, *A Short History of Twentieth-Century Technology c. 1900–c. 1950* (1982), are valuable summaries. The French equivalent to these studies is Maurice Daumas (ed.), *Histoire général des techniques*, 5 vol. (1962–79), the first 3 vol. translated as *A History of Technology and Invention: Progress Through the Ages* (1969–79). The American counterpart to the British and French works, commendably stronger than both on the social relations of technology, is Melvin Kranzberg and Carroll W. Pursell, Jr. (eds.), *Technology in Western Civilization*, 2 vol. (1967). All these general works concentrate on Western technology.

# POSTINDUSTRIAL SOCIETY

The classic work on the topic of postindustrialism is Daniel Bell, *The Coming of Post-Industrial Society: A Venture in Social Forecasting* (1973). Other informative works on the topic include Dana Fisher and William R. Freudenburg, "Postindustrialization and Environmental Quality: An Empirical Analysis of the Environmental State." *Social Forces*, 83(1):157–188 (2004); and Brian Milani, *Designing the Green Economy: The Postindustrial Alternative to Corporate Globalization* (1999).

# INDEX

changes that led to, 46–47

economic effects of, 71–75

geographic spread of, 86–87

postindustrialization, 111–114

second Industrial Revolution and changing society, 86–114

social changes and, 75–85

society before, 1–24

technological advances of, 115–152

technology in era proceeding, 25–44

industries, development of, 128–151

internal combustion engine, 124, 125, 126

iron, 23, 32, 39, 54–57, 73, 88, 129–130, 131–132, 140–141, 143

## J

Jacquard, J.M., 53

Jenner, Edward, 138

Joseph II, 17

## K

Kay, John, 22, 35, 36, 46, 51

## L

labour

condition of, 61–62

problems of capital and, 62–63

labourers/working class, social changes for, 75–76, 82–83, 103

labour unions, 68, 83–84, 106–108

landowners, 9

laissez-faire, 19–20, 50, 62

Lavoisier, Antoine, 42

Leblanc, Nicolas, 137

leisure time and habits, 77–78, 104–105, 106

Lenoir, Étienne, 124

Leonardo da Vinci, 26–28

lighting, 90, 91–93, 122–123, 128

locomotives, 58, 70, 90, 118, 119, 125, 126, 132, 142, 145

road locomotive, 143–144

Lombe brothers, 22

Louis XIV, 4, 43